MUSHROOM MAGIC

100 Fabulous Fungi Feasts and Marvellous Mushroom Meals

STEVEN WHEELER

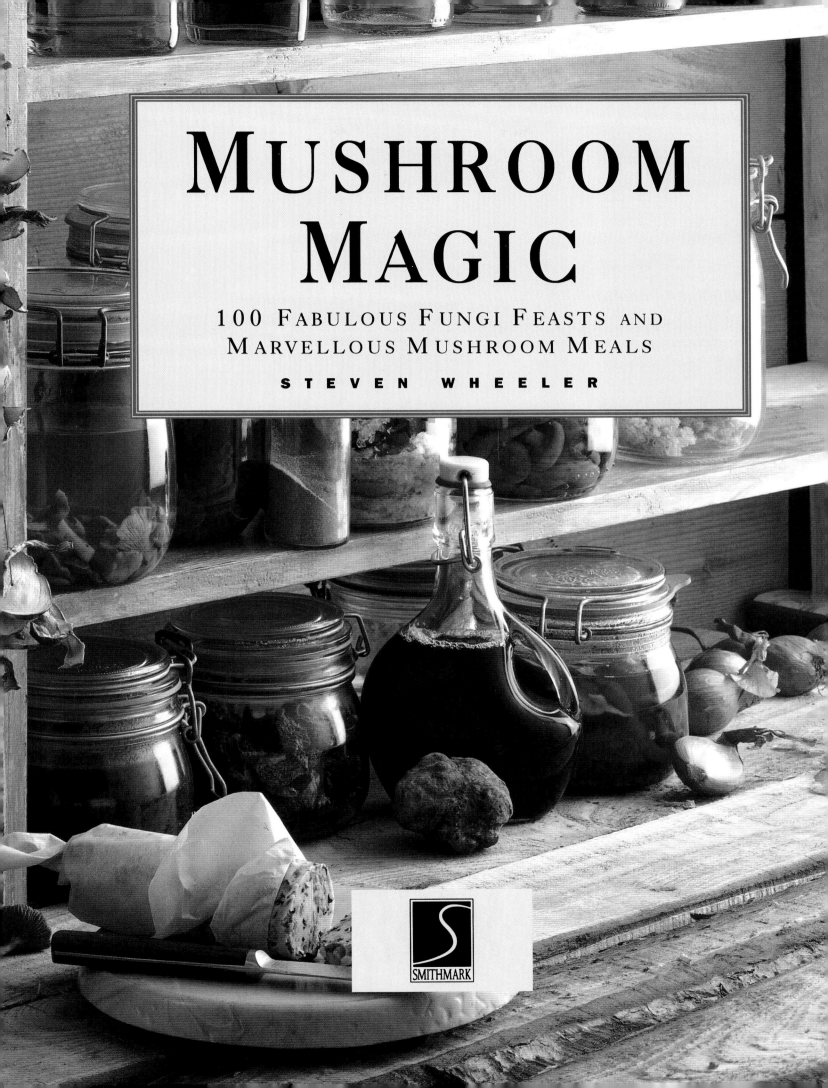

MUSHROOM MAGIC

100 Fabulous Fungi Feasts and Marvellous Mushroom Meals

STEVEN WHEELER

SMITHMARK

Publisher's Note
The publishers and authors cannot accept responsibility
for any identification of any mushroom made by users
of this guide. Although many species are edible for
many people, some species cause allergic reactions or
illness to some people: these are totally unpredictable.
Therefore, the publishers and authors cannot
take responsibility for any effects from eating any
wild mushroom.

This edition published in 1996
by SMITHMARK Publishers, a division of
U.S. Media Holdings, Inc.
16 East 32nd Street
New York, NY 10016

SMITHMARK books are available for bulk purchase,
for sales and promotion and premium use. For details
write or call the manager of special sales,
SMITHMARK Publishers Inc., 16 East 32nd Street,
New York, NY 10016; (212) 532-6600.

© Anness Publishing Ltd 1995, 1996

This book was previously published as part of a
larger compendium, *The Ultimate Mushroom Book*.

ISBN 0-8317-7323-5

Printed In Singapore By
Star Standard Industries (PTE) LTD

Contents

INTRODUCTION

From the cook's point of view, wild mushrooms are an irresistible source of flavor, texture and aroma. The recipes in this book explore the qualities of over thirty types of edible mushrooms and will show you how best to cook and enjoy them.

The passions associated with picking mushrooms are easily aroused when we realize how many good mushrooms there are growing freely in our woods and fields. Coupled with the excitement of picking mushrooms in the wild is the risk of handling poisonous varieties, such as the death cap *Amanita phalloides*, panther cap *Amanita pantherina*, yellow stainer *Agaricus xanthodermus* and destroying angel *Amanita virosa*. These often deadly poisonous mushrooms can easily be mistaken for the common and edible field mushroom *Agaricus campestris*. For your own safety, never touch a mushroom you cannot identify. When possible, accompany someone who knows which mushrooms are safe, and remember, if in doubt, don't touch them.

There are over a thousand varieties of mushroom known to be edible. The mushrooms which are best to eat are a question of taste, but it is generally agreed that the finest include the cep *Boletus edulis*, bay bolete *Boletus badius*, morel *Morchella esculenta*, chanterelle *Cantharellus cibarius* and chicken of the woods *Laetiporus sulphureus*. These mushrooms fetch a high price in the market and are sold mainly to the restaurant trade. Occasionally you may find them for sale in specialty food stores. Most precious of all is the fresh truffle which is found mainly in northern Italy and southern parts of France. Black and white truffles are found beneath the soil in mature woodland and are prized for their mysterious scent which, it is said, imitates the pheromone that causes pigs to mate.

The scent of wild mushrooms in damp woodland is enough to get most people on their knees scratching through the undergrowth. You may not be lucky enough to find a truffle, but there are many fine mushrooms to find and a home-cooked breakfast is a welcome return for the hungry mushroom picker. Even if you've only managed to find a few mushrooms, they will go a long way to flavor a plate of scrambled eggs. Parsley, thyme and fennel-scented chervil bring out their flavor as will a splash of sherry. Later in the day, wild mushrooms are ideal cooked in warming soups and broths. More delicate mushrooms are better suited to light broths.

Poultry and game taste good with mushroom flavors, either roasted, braised or sautéed. When cooking free-range chicken, try the delicate richness of the chanterelle, saffron milk-cap *Lactarius deliciosus*, hedgehog fungus *Hydnum repandum* and honey mushroom *Armillaria mellea*. Guinea fowl and pheasant carry the robust flavor of the fresh or dried cep, bay bolete, parasol mushroom and blewit. Wild duck mirrors the smoky richness of the morel and is good served with a glass of Madeira. Chicken of the woods has such a convincing taste, texture and appearance that it can be used as a substitute for chicken in chicken recipes.

Beef is a perfect match for the large field, horse and parasol mushroom. Cooked slowly with red wine, onions and a good stock, they are the making of a fine beef stew, rich and round with a luscious mushroom gravy. The delicate quality of lamb allies with the apricot sweetness of the chanterelle and saffron milk-cap. Pork belongs in a slow pot with a sauce of Jerusalem artichokes, horn of plenty *Craterellus cornucopiodes* and a purée of green olives.

The flavor of wild mushrooms is most effective with other wild foods. The sea is perhaps the most bountiful source of wild food, both fish and shellfish. Providing they are fresh (and in some cases alive), fish and shellfish are ideal ingredients to accompany wild mushrooms. When you have chosen the finest ingredients, simplicity is the best course of action, with particular care given to the preparation of sauces and garnishes. As a rule, if the fish has a delicate flavor, select a sweeter, subtle-tasting mushroom. Flat fish, such as sole, flounder and halibut suit field varieties, with a little parsley, lemon and thyme. Stronger oily fish such as salmon, tuna and trout benefit from the assertive quality of the cep, bay bolete, shiitake and blewit mushrooms.

Wild mushrooms have been valued for centuries as an alternative to meat; a delight for those who know how and where to pick them. Meat has always been expensive in the market and mushrooms have long been used to make it go further. Presently, with eating habits veering away from meat for health reasons, vegetarians are discovering again the value of wild mushrooms for their first-rate flavor and goodness. Mushrooms contain essential minerals, potassium, magnesium and iron. They are high in niacin and contain other B group vitamins. Mushrooms consist of 2–8% protein and contain around 35 calories per 4 oz. A section of this book has purely vegetarian recipes, while many recipes in the breakfast and starter sections will also appeal to vegetarians.

GOOD EDIBLE MUSHROOMS

Amanita caesarea
Caesar's mushroom

Armillaria mellea
Honey mushroom

Boletus edulis
Cep

Cantharellus cibarius
Chanterelle

Agaricus campestris and *bisporus*
Field mushroom

Boletus badius
Bay bolete

Calocybe gambosa
St George's mushroom

The assessment and value of edible mushrooms is open to opinion. Apart from the principle of putting delicate mushrooms with subtle foods and not putting mushrooms that stain black in creamy sauces, there are no rules to follow. Below is a brief and personal assessment of good edible mushrooms.

Agaricus campestris and *bisporus*
Field Mushroom
Open and closed field mushrooms provide a well-known flavor to everyday cooking. Take care when picking not to confuse this common mushroom with the poisonous yellow stainer *Agaricus xanthodermus*, destroying angel *Amanita virosa* and spring amanita *Amanita verna*.

Amanita caesarea
Caesar's Mushroom
The Caesar's mushroom is valued for

its sweet chestnut quality. It has a russet orange to yellow glow. It is not found in Britain, and is questionable in North America.

Armillaria mellea
Honey Mushroom
This is a delicious, highly perfumed mushroom. It tastes wonderful fried with eggs, or in a risotto flavored with saffron.

Boletus badius
Bay Bolete
The bay bolete shares many qualities with the cep. Young specimens are particularly good and offer a lingering richness to be enjoyed blanched in salads or cooked simply to respect their flavor.

Boletus edulis
Cep or Porcini
The cep is considered best when

small and tight. Good specimens are heavy for their size and have a butter-sweet richness when briefly sautéed. Larger ceps are best cooked in butter with a few herbs. Another bolete which is popular in the United States is the queen's bolete.

Calocybe gambosa
St George's Mushroom
The St George's mushroom has a rich meaty scent and a nutty flavor when cooked. They are very rarely found in North America, but if you do, try them with chicken and fish.

Cantharellus cibarius
Chanterelle
The intensely orange trumpet shape of the chanterelle has an appealing scent of dried apricots with a hint of citrus. Chanterelle are best tossed in nut brown butter, although their color and flavor remain true even after

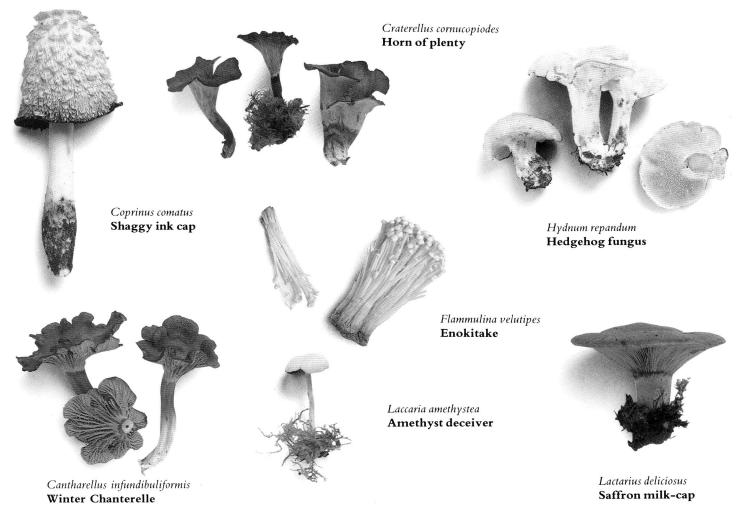

Craterellus cornucopiodes
Horn of plenty

Coprinus comatus
Shaggy ink cap

Hydnum repandum
Hedgehog fungus

Flammulina velutipes
Enokitake

Laccaria amethystea
Amethyst deceiver

Cantharellus infundibuliformis
Winter Chanterelle

Lactarius deliciosus
Saffron milk-cap

slow cooking. It is essential to avoid the false chanterelle *Hygrophoropsis aurantiaca* which can cause alarming hallucinations.

Cantharellus infundibuliformis
Winter Chanterelle
This mushroom has a rich mossy scent that combines well with other mushrooms. After trimming the base, the winter chanterelle is best used whole.

Coprinus comatus
Shaggy Ink Cap
The shaggy ink cap has a delicate flavor not unlike the field mushroom. Pick young specimens that have yet to blacken and deteriorate around the fringe. Use in smooth soups and sauces. Do not use the common ink cap *Coprinus atramentarius*, this causes a violent reaction when consumed with alcohol.

Craterellus cornucopiodes
Horn of Plenty or Black Trumpet
The horn of plenty has a sweet earthy richness that goes a long way to flavor soups, stews and casseroles. Its jet black appearance does not bleed, even after lengthy cooking.

Flammulina velutipes
Enokitake
These long-stemmed pinhead mushrooms are grown commercially on the stumps of the enoki or Chinese hackberry tree. They have a delicate flavor reminiscent of white pepper and lemon. Serve them raw or cooked in a light broth. Enokitake are available in Oriental groceries.

Hydnum repandum
Hedgehog Fungus
Young hedgehog fungus has a peppery watercress quality that is appreciated in salads. Mature specimens can be bitter and are best cooked with sweet butter and herbs.

Laccaria amethystea
Amethyst Deceiver
These distinctive grape-colored mushrooms have a subtle, gentle flavor, but provide color and interest when put with paler mushrooms.

Lactarius deliciosus
Saffron Milk-cap
The saffron milk-cap is prized for its saffron orange color and firm texture. Mature specimens often harbour insect larvae in the stem and center cap, so take care when selecting.

Laetiporus sulphureus
Chicken of the Woods or Sulphur Polypore
Chicken of the woods has an intriguing flavor and texture of roast

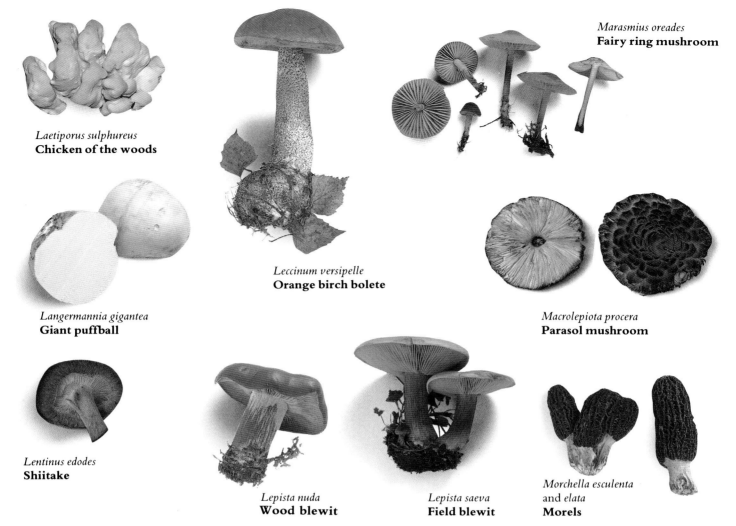

Laetiporus sulphureus
Chicken of the woods

Leccinum versipelle
Orange birch bolete

Marasmius oreades
Fairy ring mushroom

Langermannia gigantea
Giant puffball

Macrolepiota procera
Parasol mushroom

Lentinus edodes
Shiitake

Lepista nuda
Wood blewit

Lepista saeva
Field blewit

Morchella esculenta
and *elata*
Morels

chicken. When fresh, moist and fragrant, the fungus can be used to replace chicken. Another popular mushroom is hen of the woods.

Langermannia gigantea
Giant Puffball
When sliced open, the young giant puffball has a gentle meaty rich aroma similar in some ways to the cep. Older specimens discolor yellow when cut and should not be eaten.

Leccinum versipelle
Orange Birch Bolete
It has a mud spattered stem and a tawny orange cap which fades with age. It softens when cooked and provides a good texture for casseroles.

Lentinus edodes
Shiitake
Shiitake are grown commercially in the Far East on logs that are taken

from the oak related *shii* tree. They have a robust beefy sweetness that remains even after lengthy cooking.

Lepista nuda (syn. *Tricholoma nuda*)
and *Lepista saeva*
Blewit and Field Blewit
Both blewits have an assertive pine-rich perfume, that belongs with the pronounced flavor of game, toasted nuts and cheeses.

Macrolepiota procera
Parasol Mushroom
This handsome mushroom stands proudly on a tough inedible stem. Its cap offers a gamey rich flavor which strengthens when mature. Parasol mushrooms are best sautéed in butter with a few fresh herbs.

Marasmius oreades
Fairy Ring Mushroom
Fresh and dried, this common mush-

room has an oaky scent which is best cooked simply in sweet butter. Great care should be taken not to confuse the fairy ring mushroom with the deadly poisonous *Clitocybe rivulosa* and *Clitocybe dealbata*.

Morchella esculenta, vulgaris
and *elata*
Morels
The morels are the most exciting springtime fungi. Both fresh and dried morels are prized for their tobacco-rich scent of sulphur and oak. This curious scent combines especially well with eggs, beef and game. A splash of Madeira will enhance their flavor.

Pleurotus citrinopileatus
Yellow Oyster Mushroom
This pretty mushroom is designed by the mushroom cultivator to capture our attention in the supermarket.

Pleurotus ostreatus
Oyster mushroom

Pleurotus citrinopileatus
Yellow oyster mushroom

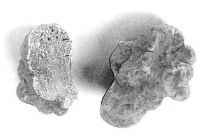

Suillus luteus
Slippery jack

Russula cyanoxantha
Charcoal burner

Sparassis crispa
Cauliflower fungus

Tuber magnatum
White truffle

Tuber aestivum
Summer truffle

However, it tastes of very little and its color disappears when cooked.

Pleurotus ostreatus
Oyster Mushroom
Both wild and cultivated oyster mushrooms have little flavor or aroma. Young specimens are best and provide bulk when combining with stronger-flavored mushrooms.

Russula cyanoxantha
Charcoal Burner
The charcoal burner is an excellent mushroom to eat. However, it is a member of a very large genus and identification can be very difficult. Correct identification is essential because some are poisonous.

Sparassis crispa
Cauliflower Fungus
The cauliflower fungus is known more for its texture than its flavor.

When raw and dried it has a curious scent of latex and ammonia which goes after brief cooking. The crisp texture is appreciated when combined with other mushrooms.

Suillus luteus (syn. *Boletus luteus*)
Slippery Jack or Pine Bolete
The slippery jack, so named because of its gluten covered cap, tends to absorb moisture in wet weather. When cooked, it softens to provide a basis for smooth soups and sauces.

Tricholoma ponderosa
White Matsutake
Not known in Europe, it is common in North America. It has an interesting flavor.

Tuber aestivum
Summer Truffle
Less intensely flavored than the white truffle, this warty black variety has a

more delicate aroma associated with oak woodlands rather than the farm. More robust in texture than its white counterpart, the summer truffle should be pared before slicing raw. Truffles benefit from a few drops of truffle oil added towards the end of cooking.

Tuber magnatum
Piedmont or White Truffle
This rare and expensive tuber is found in very limited areas, mostly in northern Italy. It has a strong and curious aroma connected with the intensity of a pig sty! To touch, the white truffle has the fragility of firm fresh yeast. Unfortunately highly trained dogs or pigs are needed to find it. If you are fortunate enough to come by a white truffle, scrub it clean and shave over plainly cooked food. The flavor of the white truffle goes if it is cooked.

Drying Mushrooms

The process of drying mushrooms intensifies individual flavors and aromas. The cep develops a pronounced beefy, rich aroma with a chamois leather sweetness. The bay boletes have a more pronounced sweetness and a less complex aroma. The morel develops a sulphur-rich, beefy, almost smoky quality, while fairy rings have a gentle sweetness. The cauliflower fungus has a strong latex vinegar smell which disappears with cooking. The saffron milk-cap and chanterelle have a fruity richness and the horn of plenty has a dark sweet woodland flavor.

When fully dried, mushrooms will keep through the winter in air-tight jars, providing a useful and nutritious source of flavor for soups, stews and casseroles.

1 To make sure the mushrooms are free from infestation, wipe them with a damp cloth, but avoid washing, and cut away damaged parts. Slice the mushrooms thinly. When drying chanterelles, remove the stems of small specimens as they tend to toughen.

3 (*Right*) When mushrooms are completely dry, place each variety in an air-tight jar, label and store in a dark place. If mushrooms are not fully dry before storing, molds will grow and spoil your work.

2 Lay the mushrooms on a basket tray, or baking sheet lined with several layers of newspaper and a final layer of baking parchment. Put in a warm and well-ventilated place for two days. For fast drying, preheat an oven with fan to 150°F, keep the door ajar and dry the mushrooms for 2 hours. If you have a small quantity of mushrooms, thread them with needle and thread and hang up to dry.

Mushroom Powder

The intense flavor of dried mushrooms can be used in powder form to enliven winter soups, stews and curries. The curry-scented milk-cap, *Lactarius camphoratus*, offers a pungent reminder of fenugreek and should always be used sparingly. The anise mushroom, *Clitocybe odora* is another powerful substitute for spices and can be used in sweet and savory cooking. Other mushrooms suitable for powdering include many of the boletes and field and horse mushrooms.

1 Wipe clean the inside of a coffee grinder with a dry cloth. Put in the well-dried mushrooms and reduce to a fine powder.

2 Transfer to an air-tight jar, label and keep in a dark place. Use sparingly.

To Reconstitute Dried Mushrooms

To bring dried mushrooms back to life, they need to be soaked in warm water for 20 minutes. Boiling water will make them tough. The water used to soak dried mushrooms should be saved and added to stocks.

1 Place the mushrooms in a bowl. Cover with warm water and let stand for 20 minutes.

Salt Preserving

Salt preserving is an age-old method of keeping mushrooms, and is still used in countries of the former Soviet Union. The method eliminates bacterial growth by packing mushrooms with layers of salt. The salt draws out the moisture in the mushrooms, forming a brine. Before using, the mushrooms need to be soaked in plenty of cold water to reduce saltiness. After soaking, salt preserved mushrooms can be added to braised meats such as beef, pork and tripe.

Suitable mushrooms for salting include: hedgehog fungus, oyster mushroom, bay bolete, winter chanterelle, saffron milk-cap and wood blewit.

The proportion of salt to mushrooms is 3–1.

1 (Right) Wipe the mushrooms clean with a damp cloth, trim and ensure that they are free from grit and infestation. Slice the mushrooms thickly with a stainless steel knife. Place a layer of rock or sea salt in the bottom of a covered glass or stoneware jar, layer with mushrooms. Alternate with more salt and mushrooms until full.

2 After 3–4 hours, you will find the volume of mushrooms will drop as the salt draws out their moisture. At this stage additional layers of salt and mushrooms can be added. Salted mushrooms will keep safely in a cool place for up to 12 months.

Freezing Mushrooms

To preserve mushrooms quickly and effectively, consider freezing them. Firmer varieties are best, such as shiitake, blewits, horn of plenty, chanterelle, closed field and horse mushrooms. To thaw, take Antonio Carluccio's advice and immerse briefly in boiling water before using.

1 Bring a saucepan of salted water to the boil and line a tray with greaseproof paper. Ensure mushrooms are free from grit and infestation then trim and slice thickly if large. Drop the mushrooms into the boiling water and simmer for 1 minute.

2 Drain well and open freeze for 30–40 minutes on a paper-lined tray. When frozen, turn loosely into plastic bags, label and return to the freezer for up to 6 months.

Preserving Mushrooms in Butter

Capturing the flavor and aroma of wild mushrooms in butter is a favorite method of preserving. The finest *Boletus*, *B. edulis*, *B. badius* and *B. pruinatus*, retain their qualities best when softened and combined with unsalted butter. If you are lucky enough to chance upon a few fresh truffles, these also keep well, peeled, chopped and concealed raw in butter. Other mushrooms that keep well in butter include the morel, chanterelle, saffron milk-cap and Caesar's mushroom. Wild mushroom butter is delicious melted over simply cooked meat or fish. It is also good over pasta, or in soups, sauces and gravies.

1 lb / 4½ cups mushrooms
¾ cup unsalted butter
½ oz / ½ cup fresh black or white truffle, peeled and chopped (optional), or 3 drops truffle oil (optional)

1 Be sure the mushrooms are free from grit and infestation. Trim, slice and chop. Melt 2 oz / 4 tbsp of the butter in a large nonstick frying pan. Add the mushrooms and sauté over a gentle heat to reduce the volume, then simmer in their own juices for 2–3 minutes. Cool.

2 Combine the cooked mushrooms and truffles, or oil if you are using this instead, with the remaining butter and spoon the mixture onto a square of greaseproof paper.

3 (*Right*) Roll into a cigar shape, twist each end and label. Refrigerate for up to 10 days or freeze for up to 8 weeks.

Duxelle

Duxelle is a preparation known in classical French cooking. It consists of finely chopped mushrooms and shallots cooked in butter, wine and herbs, and forms the basis for many well-known soups, sauces, stuffings, gratins and fillings. The name, according to Larousse, derives from a small town in the north east of France called Uxel. The preparation may be credited to La Varenne who cooked for the household of the Marquis d'Uxelles in the 17th century. Duxelle can be made from wild or cultivated mushrooms and refrigerated or frozen in ice cube portions for 10 days or 8 weeks respectively.

4 tbsp unsalted butter
2 shallots, chopped
1 lb / 4½ cups wild and/or cultivated mushrooms, trimmed and finely chopped
1 sprig thyme, chopped
3½ tbsp white wine or sherry
celery salt
freshly ground black pepper

1 Melt the butter in a large nonstick frying pan over a gentle heat, add the shallots and sauté for 2–3 minutes to soften without browning.

2 (*Right*) Add the mushrooms, thyme and wine and simmer so that the mushroom juices run, then increase the heat to boil off the moisture. When quite dry, season with celery salt and pepper, if using right away. Otherwise, cool and refrigerate or freeze.

Mushroom Purée

Mushroom purée takes Duxelle a stage further and reduces it to a fine purée. Mushroom purée is used mainly for the enrichment of soups and sauces, although a spoonful works wonders in a casserole of beef or game. As with the Duxelle, mushroom purée freezes conveniently in ice cube portions.

1 Prepare the Duxelle as shown in the previous recipe. Spoon into a food processor and blend until smooth.

2 Allow to cool, transfer into an airtight jar and refrigerate for up to 10 days or freeze for up to 8 weeks.

Mushroom Extract

The finest edible mushrooms are best preserved whole or sliced. More common although less elegant species such as the field, horse and parasol mushroom lend their flavor and color to a dark extract. It is very important to ensure mushrooms are properly identified before using. An incorrectly identified mushroom put among the others can cause fatal illness. Shaggy ink caps are worth putting in, as are any overgrown boletus mushrooms providing they are free from infestation and are in good condition. Any deterioration can cause the extract to ferment at a later date. The flavor extracted from the mushrooms will keep in the refrigerater in a screw-top jar or bottle for 8–10 weeks. Use readily to enliven and enrich winter soups, stews and game dishes.

1 lb / 4½ cups field, horse and parasol mushrooms, shaggy ink caps, honey mushrooms, slippery jack and/or winter chanterelles, trimmed and roughly chopped
1¼ cups water
⅞ cup red wine
4 tbsp dark soy sauce
1 tsp salt
1 sprig thyme

1 Place all the ingredients in a large stainless steel pan. Bring to a boil and simmer uncovered for 45 minutes.

2 Strain the mushrooms through a fine mesh strainer, pressing as much liquid as possible back into the pan. Return the extract to the boil and reduce to half its volume.

3 *(Left)* Sterilize a preserving jar or bottle by immersing it in boiling water for a few minutes. Drain. Fill the jar or bottle with the mushroom liquid, cover and allow to cool. When cool, label and store in the refrigerator. Mushroom extract can be frozen and used in ice cube portions.

Pickled Mushrooms

The principle of pickling eliminates the chance of bacterial growth by immersing mushrooms in vinegar. Vinegar can be flavored and diluted to lessen the sharp taste. In this recipe shiitake mushrooms take on an oriental flavor, although other firm mushrooms and spices can also be used. It is best to dress pickled mushrooms with olive oil when serving, to restore balance. Serve as an appetizer or buffet style lunch item.

1 cup white wine vinegar
2/3 cup water
1 tsp salt
1 red chili
2 tsp coriander seeds
2 tsp szechuan pepper or anise-pepper
9 oz / 3 cups shiitake mushrooms, halved if large

1 Bring the wine vinegar and water to a simmer in a stainless steel pan. Add the salt, chili, coriander, szechuan pepper or anise-pepper and mushrooms and cook for 10 minutes.

2 Sterilize a 2¼ cup preserving jar by immersing in boiling water. Drain until dry. Transfer mushrooms and liquid to the jar, seal, label and leave for at least 10 days before trying.

Chanterelle Vodka

If you manage to find a few chanterelles on your mushroom foray, consider steeping them in vodka. Vodka has a neutral flavor and allows the apricot quality of the chanterelles to shine. Chill thoroughly before serving as an aperitif.

1½ cups vodka
3 oz / 1 cup young chanterelle mushrooms, trimmed

1 Place the chanterelle mushrooms in a clean preserving bottle or jar.

2 Pour in the vodka, cover and leave at room temperature. Chanterelle vodka is ready when the mushrooms have dropped to the bottom.

Preserving Mushrooms in Oil

The method of preserving in oil is ideally suited to good quality firm mushrooms. The process can seem expensive, but the oil used takes on a delicious mushroom flavor which can then be used to make special salad dressings.

1 cup white wine vinegar
⅔ cup water
1 tsp salt
1 sprig thyme
½ bay leaf
1 red chili (optional)
1 lb / 4½ cups assorted wild mushrooms, including young bay bolete, chanterelles, saffron milk-caps and horn of plenty, trimmed and halved if large
1⅔ cups virgin olive oil

1 Bring the vinegar and water to a simmer in a stainless steel pan. Add the salt, thyme, bay leaf and chili if using, and infuse for 15 minutes.

2 Add the mushrooms and simmer for 10 minutes. Sterilize a 2¼ cup preserving jar by immersing in boiling water. Drain until dry. Lift the cooked mushrooms out of the liquid, drain well and place in the jar.

3 (*Right*) Cover the mushrooms with oil, close the lid and label. Mushrooms in oil will keep in a cool place for up to 12 months.

Spiced Mushrooms in Alcohol

Winter chanterelles and oyster mushrooms combine with caraway seeds, lemon and chili to make this unusual and warming infusion.

3 oz / 1 cup winter chanterelle and oyster mushrooms
1 tsp caraway seeds
1 lemon
1 red chili
1½ cups vodka

1 Place the mushrooms, caraway seeds, lemon and chili in a clean preserving jar or bottle.

2 Pour in the vodka and leave for 2–3 weeks until the mushrooms no longer float. Chill thoroughly and serve as an aperitif.

Wild Mushroom Breakfasts

Kedgeree of Oyster and Chanterelle Mushrooms

Providing breakfast for an army of late risers is quite a challenge. This delicious kedgeree combines the rich woodland flavor of oyster and chanterelle mushrooms with eggs, rice and a touch of curry seasoning.

SERVES 4

2 tbsp butter
1 medium onion, chopped
2 cups long grain rice
1 small carrot, cut into julienne strips
3¾ cups chicken or vegetable stock, boiling
1 pinch saffron
8 oz / 2½ cups oyster and chanterelle mushrooms, trimmed and halved
4 oz floury potato, peeled and grated
1⅞ cup milk
½ chicken or vegetable stock cube
½ tsp curry paste
2 tbsp heavy cream
4 eggs
4 tbsp chopped fresh parsley

Cook's Tip
Kedgeree will keep warm without spoiling in a covered dish for up to 2 hours.

1 Melt the butter in a large saucepan, add the onion and fry it gently without letting it color.

2 Turn half of the softened onion into a medium-sized saucepan. Put the rice, carrot and stock in the large pan, add a pinch of saffron, stir and simmer, uncovered for 15 minutes. Remove the pan from the heat, cover and stand for 5 minutes.

3 Add the oyster and chanterelle mushrooms to the pan with the onion and cook gently for a few minutes to soften. Add the grated potato, milk, stock cube and curry paste and simmer for 15 minutes until the potatoes have thickened the liquid.

4 Place the eggs in a pan of boiling water and cook for 10 minutes. Run them under cold water to cool, then peel and cut into quarters.

5 Fork the rice onto a warmed serving platter. Spoon the mushrooms and sauce into the center and garnish with the egg quarters and chopped parsley.

Cook's Tip
There are many varieties of long grain rice available. The least flavorsome are the non-stick brands that have been part cooked to remove a proportion of starch. The notion that every grain of rice must be separate undermines the nature and flavor of good rice.

Apricot Chanterelle Breakfast Muffins

Smell a chanterelle and you will be reminded of apricots. To encourage this association, here is a recipe for chanterelle muffins flecked with dried apricots and topped with pine nuts.

MAKES 12
1⅓ cups self-rising flour
½ tsp salt
1 tbsp chopped dried apricots
3 oz / 1 cup chanterelle mushrooms, trimmed and chopped
1 tsp chopped fresh thyme
1 egg
4 tbsp butter, melted
½ cup milk
¼ cup pine nuts or sliced almonds
melted butter or oil for brushing

1 Preheat the oven to 425°F. Grease 12 deep muffin tins with butter or oil and set aside.

2 Sift the flour and salt into a bowl. Add the apricots, mushrooms, thyme, egg, butter and milk, then stir to make a thick batter.

3 Spoon the mixture into the prepared muffin tins, so they are about two-thirds full. Sprinkle with pine nuts and bake near the top of the oven for 12 minutes until golden, then turn out and serve warm. They are particularly delicious cut in half and spread with butter.

Egg, Bacon and Wild Mushroom Fry Up

When you arrive home tired and hungry after a mushroom hunt, a quick fry up will restore your strength and vitality.

SERVES 4
6 tbsp goose fat or lard
12 oz bacon
1 lb pork sausages
12 oz / 3½ cups assorted wild mushrooms
PALE: oyster and parasol mushrooms, hedgehog fungus, fairy ring and honey mushrooms, ceps, chanterelles and chicken of the woods.
DARK: field mushrooms, shaggy ink caps, horn of plenty and queen boletes
1 sprig thyme
salt and freshly ground black pepper
4 eggs
4 slices brown or white bread
butter for spreading

1 Preheat the oven to 300°F. Melt 2 tbsp of the fat in a large nonstick frying pan and fry the bacon and sausages. Transfer to a serving dish and keep warm.

Cook's Tip
If using both pale and dark mushrooms, it is best to cook them separately, one batch at a time.

2 Clean the mushrooms and slice if necessary. Add to the pan and toss in the fat, then add the thyme and cook for 2–3 minutes. Season with salt and pepper, transfer to a bowl, cover and keep warm.

3 Melt the remaining fat in the pan and fry the eggs. Meanwhile toast the bread and spread with butter. Serve with the bacon, sausages and mushrooms.

Toasted Brioche, Scrambled Eggs and Morels

Morels have a rich flavor that combines well with other rich ingredients such as eggs, cream and Madeira. This simple breakfast dish can be made with fresh or dried morels.

SERVES 4

5 oz / 1½ cups fresh morels or ½ oz / ¼ cup dried
2 tbsp unsalted butter
1 shallot, finely chopped
4 tbsp Madeira
4 tbsp crème fraîche
4 small brioches

For the Scrambled Eggs

8 eggs
4 tbsp crème fraîche
salt and freshly ground black pepper
2 tbsp unsalted butter

1 If using dried morels, cover with warm water, soak for 20 minutes and drain. Melt the butter in a non stick frying pan and gently fry the shallot until it is softened. Add the morels and cook briefly, then stir in the Madeira and cook until the liquid is syrupy. Stir in the crème fraîche and simmer briefly. Season, transfer to a bowl and keep warm.

2 Remove the tops from the brioches and toast under a moderate broiler.

Cook's Tip
Madeira provides an oaky hazelnut flavor to balance stronger-tasting mushrooms. You can also use a medium dry sherry.

3 Break the eggs into a bowl, add the crème fraîche, season and beat with a fork. Melt the butter in the frying pan, pour in the eggs and cook, stirring gently but continuously until the eggs are slightly cooked. Remove from the heat: the eggs will continue cooking in their own heat.

4 Spoon the scrambled eggs over the brioches and top with morels.

English Muffins with a Florentine Parasol Topping

The parasol mushroom is prized for its delicate texture and rich flavor. The stems of open specimens are tough but both the stem and cap of closed parasols are delicious with a creamy spinach topping.

SERVES 4

14 oz young leaf spinach, stems removed
salt and freshly ground black pepper
12 oz / 3½ cups parasol mushroom caps
4 tbsp unsalted butter, plus extra for spreading
½ garlic clove, crushed
5 sprigs thyme
1 cup crème fraîche
pinch of grated nutmeg
4 English muffins, split

1 Rinse the spinach in plenty of water, then place in a large saucepan with a pinch of salt. Cover and cook over a steady heat for 6–8 minutes, then drain in a colander, pressing out as much water as you can with the back of a spoon. Chop the spinach finely.

2 Chop the mushrooms, with stems if small, very finely, then melt the butter in a frying pan and add the mushrooms together with the garlic and 1 sprig of thyme. Cook for 3–4 minutes then add the chopped spinach and ⅔ cup of the crème fraîche. Season with salt, pepper and a pinch of nutmeg. Toast the muffins, split and spread lightly with butter.

3 Spoon the spinach mixture onto the muffins, top with the remaining crème fraîche and garnish with thyme.

Cook's Tip
If using frozen chopped spinach, allow half the weight of fresh spinach, defrost thoroughly and squeeze dry.

Parsley, Lemon and Garlic Mushrooms on Toast

Field mushrooms have a long and happy relationship with garlic, but too often the intense flavor of the garlic takes over. With respect for the mushroom, the garlic in this recipe is tempered with a generous amount of fresh parsley and a touch of lemon.

SERVES 4

2 tbsp unsalted butter, plus extra for spreading
1 medium onion, chopped
1 garlic clove, crushed
12 oz / 3½ cups assorted wild mushrooms such as field mushrooms, shaggy ink caps and honey mushrooms, trimmed and sliced
3 tbsp dry sherry
5 tbsp chopped fresh parsley
1 tbsp lemon juice
salt and freshly ground black pepper
4 slices brown or white bread

Cook's Tip
Italian parsley has a good flavor and keeps well in the refrigerator. To keep it fresh, stand in a jar of water and cover with a plastic bag.

1 Melt the butter in a large nonstick frying pan and gently sauté the onion without letting it color.

2 Add the garlic and mushrooms, cover and cook for 3–5 minutes. Add the sherry, cook uncovered to evaporate the liquid.

3 Stir in the parsley and lemon juice, and then season to taste with salt and pepper.

4 Toast the bread and spread with butter. Spoon the mushrooms over the toast and serve.

Hedgehog Mushroom Pancakes with Chive Butter

Pancakes are an ideal base for subtly flavored wild mushrooms. Pale varieties, in particular the peppery hedgehog fungus, work best and should be softened in butter before they are added to the batter.

MAKES 12 PANCAKES

4 tbsp unsalted butter
9 oz / 3¼ cups hedgehog fungus, trimmed and chopped
2 oz hedgehog fungus, sliced

For the Pancakes

1½ cups self-rising flour
salt and white pepper
2 eggs
⅞ cup milk

For the Chive Butter

scant 1 cup fresh finely chopped chives
½ cup unsalted butter, softened
1 tsp lemon juice

1 First make the chive butter. Stir the chopped chives and lemon juice into the butter. Turn out onto a 10 in square of wax paper and form into a sausage. Roll up, twist both ends of the paper and chill in the fridge for about an hour until it is firm.

2 Melt half of the butter in a large pan, add the chopped mushrooms and sauté over a moderate heat, allowing the mushrooms to soften and the moisture to evaporate. Spread onto a tray and cool. Cook the sliced mushrooms in a pat of butter and set aside.

3 To make the batter, sift the flour and salt and pepper into a bowl. Beat the eggs into the milk and add to the flour, stirring to make a thick batter. Add the chopped mushrooms.

4 Heat the remaining butter in the pan, arrange five slices of mushrooms at a time in the bottom, then spoon the batter into 2 in circles over each mushroom. When bubbles appear on the surface, turn the pancakes over and cook for another 10–15 seconds. Serve warm with slices of chive butter.

Miso Shiitake Breakfast Soup

This Japanese breakfast soup provides a light nourishing start to the day. It is flavored with shiitake mushrooms and a soy protein called miso. Both are available from health food stores.

SERVES 4

3 shiitake mushrooms, fresh or dried
5 cups water, boiling
3 tbsp light miso paste
4 oz bean curd (tofu), cut into large dice
1 scallion, green part only, sliced

1 If using dried mushrooms, soak in warm water for 20 minutes then drain. Slice the mushrooms thinly. Pour the boiling water into a saucepan. Stir in the miso, add the mushrooms and simmer for 5 minutes.

2 Divide the bean curd among four warmed soup bowls, ladle in the broth, scatter with sliced scallion and serve.

Cook's Tip
Miso is a fermented soybean paste that varies in strength and color according to the maturity of the soybeans.

Home-baked Chanterelle Croissant

Chanterelle mushrooms will make a delicious filling and can be added to quick-bake croissants for an unusual and satisfying breakfast. The filling can be made well in advance and goes a long way.

SERVES 4

2 tbsp unsalted butter
4 oz / 1¼ cups fresh chanterelle mushrooms, trimmed and sliced, or ½ oz / ¼ cup dried, soaked in warm water, drained and sliced
4 tbsp heavy cream
1 tbsp medium sherry or Madeira
salt and freshly ground black pepper
1 package quick-bake croissants
1 egg, beaten

1 Preheat the oven as directed on the package for the croissants. Melt the butter in a saucepan, add the chanterelles and sauté gently for 3–4 minutes to soften without letting them color. Add the cream and sherry, increase the heat and allow the moisture to evaporate. Season to taste and cool.

Cook's Tip
Other firm mushrooms can be used as a filling for the croissants. They might include ceps, bay bolete, winter chanterelles, morel, saffron milk caps, hedgehog fungus, field and horse mushrooms, oyster and matsukake mushrooms.

2 Lay the croissant dough shapes out on a floured surface. Place a spoonful of the mixture at the wide end of each triangle. Brush the pointed end of each triangle with beaten egg and roll up, enclosing the filling.

3 Arrange the croissants on a baking sheet, brush with a little more beaten egg and bake in the oven according to instructions on the package. Serve warm.

Mushrooms in a Tarragon Cream Sauce

When your search for wild mushrooms yields only a few specimens and you have to provide breakfast for the proverbial five thousand, combine what you have with a few cultivated mushrooms – enhanced here in a creamy tarragon sauce.

SERVES 4

4 tbsp unsalted butter, plus extra for spreading
2 shallots, finely chopped
2–8 oz / ½–3 cups wild mushrooms such as hen of the woods, honey mushrooms, chanterelles, winter chanterelles, ceps, chicken of the woods, parasol mushrooms or hedgehog fungus, trimmed and sliced
12 oz / 3½ cups Cremini mushrooms, trimmed and sliced
⅔ cup heavy cream
3 tbsp chopped fresh tarragon
4 slices brown or white bread

1 Melt the butter in a large nonstick frying pan, add the shallots and sauté over a gentle heat until they are soft, without letting them color.

Cook's Tip
Almost any variety of mushrooms can be used in a cream sauce, but do avoid dark specimens which can turn the sauce gray.

2 Add your chosen mushrooms and cook over a moderate heat to soften. Add the cream and tarragon, increase the heat and cook until thick and creamy.

3 Toast the bread and spread with butter. Spoon over the mushroom mixture and serve at once.

Saffron Milk-caps with Parsley, Butter and Pine Nuts

Serving wild mushrooms on toast is a quick, easy way to appreciate their individual flavors. Butter-fried saffron milk caps are good, served with a handful of chopped parsley and a sprinkling of toasted pine nuts.

SERVES 4

¼ cup pine nuts
1 tsp vegetable oil
4 tbsp unsalted butter, plus extra for spreading
1 shallot, finely chopped
12 oz / 3½ cups saffron milk-caps, trimmed and sliced
3 tbsp heavy cream
5 tbsp chopped fresh parsley
salt and freshly ground black pepper
4 slices brown or white bread

1 Sauté the pine nuts in the oil, tilting the pan, and brown over a moderate heat. Set aside.

2 Soften the shallot in half the butter. Add the mushrooms and remaining butter and cook until soft. Stir in the cream and cook until thick. Stir in the parsley and season to taste.

3 Toast the bread and spread with butter. Spoon the mushroom mixture over the toast, sprinkle with toasted pine nuts and serve.

Cook's Tip
Saffron milk caps have hollow stems which can harbor insect larvae. Be sure to avoid any that are infested.

Bacon, Egg and Chanterelle Sandwiches

When mid-morning hunger strikes, few mushroom hunters can resist a plate of egg and bacon sandwiches stuffed with chanterelles.

SERVES 4

12 oz bacon
4 tbsp unsalted butter, plus extra for spreading
4 oz / 1¼ cups chanterelle mushrooms, trimmed and halved
4 tbsp peanut oil
4 eggs
4 large whole grain rolls, split
salt and freshly ground black pepper

1 Place the bacon in a large nonstick frying pan and sauté in its own fat until crisp. Transfer to a plate, cover and keep warm.

Cook's Tip
For best effect, let the aroma of frying bacon and mushrooms fill the breakfast room.

2 Melt 2 tbsp of the butter in the pan, add the chanterelles and sauté gently until soft without letting them color. Transfer to a plate, cover and keep warm.

3 Melt the remaining butter, add the oil and heat to a moderate temperature. Break the eggs into the pan and fry as you like them, sunny side up or over easy.

4 Toast the rolls, spread with butter, then layer with bacon, chanterelles and a fried egg. Season, top with the second half of the roll and serve.

Chicken of the Woods Cornbread with Bacon and Tomatoes

Savory cornbread is a welcome sight at breakfast time and is really delicious with crispy broiled bacon and tomatoes.

SERVES 4

2 tbsp butter
2 oz / ¾ cup chicken of the woods, trimmed and finely chopped
1 cup all-purpose flour
¾ cup fine cornmeal
2 tsp baking powder
½ tsp salt
½ tsp sugar
⅔ cup milk
2 eggs
3 oz corn, canned or frozen
12 oz bacon
4 tomatoes, halved
salt and freshly ground black pepper
1 bunch watercress, to garnish

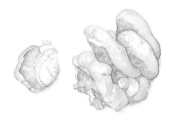

1 Preheat oven to 400°F. Melt the butter in a frying pan, add the chicken of the woods and sauté over a low heat for 5 minutes, then set aside to cool. Lightly oil a 3¾ cup loaf pan then line with wax paper.

2 Sift the flour, cornmeal, baking powder, salt and sugar into a bowl. Add the milk, eggs, corn and mushrooms. Stir to make batter.

3 Preheat the broiler to a moderate temperature. Meanwhile, turn the batter into the prepared pan and bake near the top of the oven for 25 minutes. Allow to cool slightly.

Cook's Tip

For individual shapes, spoon the cornbread mixture into greased muffin tins and bake for 10–12 minutes at 425°F.

4 Arrange the bacon and tomato halves on a tray or broiler pan and season the tomatoes with salt and pepper. Broil until the bacon is golden, turning once.

5 Lift the cornbread out of the pan and cut into thick slices. Serve with the broiled bacon and tomatoes, garnished with watercress.

Champagne Truffle Breakfast

When you have something to celebrate, start the day with a stylish breakfast. Scrambled eggs with fresh truffles are a treat with toasted brioche and Champagne. For the best flavor, it is worth tracking down fresh black and white truffles. Preserved truffles offer little if any flavor and benefit from a drop or two of truffle oil.

SERVES 4
4 brioches
8 fresh farm eggs
4 tbsp crème fraîche
3 drops truffle oil (optional)
salt and freshly ground black pepper
1 fresh black truffle
2 tbsp unsalted butter, plus extra for spreading
Champagne, to serve

1 Preheat a moderate broiler. Slice the brioche, toast and keep warm.

2 Break the eggs into a bowl, add the crème fraîche and truffle oil, if using, season and beat with a fork. Then slice half of the truffle finely into the egg mixture.

3 Melt the butter in the frying pan, pour in the eggs and with a flat wooden spoon stir around the base of the pan until lightly scrambled.

4 Butter the toasted brioches and arrange on four plates.

5 Spoon the scrambled egg onto each slice of brioche and scatter with truffle shavings. Serve with Champagne.

Cook's Tip
To ensure scrambled eggs are soft and creamy, they should be taken off the heat while a little underdone.

Cook's Tip
When using truffle oil, never be tempted to add more than a few drops. If too much of this precious oil is used its flavor will become bitter to taste.

Soups, Starters & Salads

Buckwheat Blinis with Mushroom Caviar

These little Russian pancakes are traditionally served with fish roe caviar and soured cream. The term caviar is also given to fine vegetable mixtures called ikry. This wild mushroom ikry caviar is popular in the autumn and has a silky rich texture.

SERVES 4

1 cup all-purpose flour
1/3 cup buckwheat flour
1/2 tsp salt
1 1/4 cups milk
1 tsp dry yeast
2 eggs, separated

For the Caviar

12 oz / 3 1/2 cups mixed assorted wild mushrooms such as field mushrooms, queen bolete, bay boletes, oyster and honey mushrooms
1 tsp celery salt
2 tbsp walnut oil
1 tbsp lemon juice
3 tbsp chopped fresh parsley
freshly ground black pepper
scant 1 cup sour cream or crème fraîche

1 To make the caviar, trim and chop the mushrooms, then place them in a glass bowl, toss with the celery salt and cover with a weighted plate.

2 Let the mushrooms stand for 2 hours until the juices have run out into the bottom of the bowl. Rinse the mushrooms thoroughly to remove the salt, drain and press out as much liquid as you can with the back of a spoon. Return them to the bowl and toss with walnut oil, lemon juice, parsley and a twist of pepper. Chill.

3 Sift the two flours together with the salt in a large mixing bowl. Heat the milk to approximately body temperature. Add the yeast, stirring until dissolved, then pour into the flour, add the egg yolks and stir to make a smooth batter. Cover with a damp cloth and leave in a warm place.

4 Whisk the egg whites in a clean bowl until stiff, then fold into the risen batter.

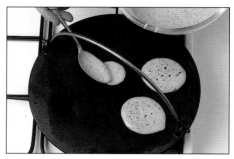

5 Heat a cast-iron pan or griddle to a moderate temperature. Moisten with oil, then drop spoonfuls of the batter onto the surface. When bubbles rise to the surface, turn them over and cook briefly on the other side. Spoon on the sour cream, top with the mushroom caviar and serve.

Wild Mushroom Tapenade Toasts

Tapenade is a paste made from black olives, garlic, anchovies, capers, olive oil and lemon. A little goes a long way. Here it is spread on bread, toasted and topped with wild mushrooms and hard-boiled eggs.

SERVES 4

12 oz / 3½ cups strongly flavored wild mushrooms such as ceps, bay boletes, chicken of the woods, saffron milk-caps and chanterelles, trimmed and sliced
4 tbsp unsalted butter
½ lemon
salt and freshly ground black pepper
4 small eggs
1 French loaf, sliced
1 small bunch parsley, to garnish
For the Tapenade
5 oz / 1 cup Kalamata olives, pitted
1 garlic clove, peeled
5 anchovy fillets
1 tbsp capers
2 tbsp olive oil
juice of ½ lemon

Cook's Tip
If you don't have time to make your own tapenade, buy it ready-made from delicatessens and specialist food stores.

1 Sauté the mushrooms gently in butter for 6–8 minutes to soften, then increase heat to evaporate the juices. Add a generous squeeze of lemon and season to taste. Transfer to a bowl, cover and keep warm.

3 Preheat a broiler to a moderate temperature. Meanwhile cool the eggs under running cold water, peel and cut into quarters. Then slice the French loaf diagonally and toast on one side. Spread the other side thinly with tapenade and toast again.

2 To make the tapenade, place all the tapenade ingredients in a food processor and blend to a fine paste. Boil the eggs for 10 minutes.

4 Heap each piece of toast with wild mushrooms, top with a section of hard-boiled egg and garnish with a sprig of parsley.

French Onion and Morel Soup

French onion soup is appreciated for its light beefy taste. Few improvements can be made to this classic soup, but a few richly scented morel mushrooms will impart a worthwhile flavor.

SERVES 4

4 tbsp unsalted butter, plus extra for spreading
1 tbsp vegetable oil
3 medium onions, sliced
3¾ cups beef stock
5 tbsp Madeira or sherry
8 medium dried morel mushrooms
4 slices French bread
1 cup Gruyère, Beaufort or Fontina cheese, grated
2 tbsp chopped fresh parsley

1 Melt the butter and oil in a large frying pan, add the onions and cook for 10–15 minutes until the onions are a rich mahogany brown color.

Cook's Tip
The flavor and richness of this soup will improve with keeping. Refrigerate for up to 5 days.

2 Transfer the browned onions to a large saucepan, cover with beef stock, add the Madeira and the morels, then simmer for 20 minutes.

3 Preheat the broiler to a moderate temperature and toast the French bread on both sides. Spread one side with butter and heap with grated cheese. Ladle the soup into four flameproof bowls, float the cheese toasts on top and broil until crisp and brown. Alternatively, broil the cheese-topped toast, place one slice in each warmed soup bowl and ladle the hot soup over. The toast will float to the surface. Sprinkle with chopped parsley and serve.

Cep Soup with Parsley Croutons

The lasting aroma of the cep mushroom is caught in this delicious soup.

SERVES 4

4 tbsp unsalted butter
2 medium onions, finely chopped
1 garlic clove
8 oz / 2½ cups fresh ceps or bay bolete, sliced, or 1 oz / ½ cup dried
5 tbsp dry white wine
3¾ cups chicken stock, boiling
4 oz floury potatoes, peeled and diced
1 sprig thyme
1 tbsp lemon juice
salt and freshly ground black pepper

For the Croutons

3 slices day-old bread
4 tbsp butter
3 tbsp finely chopped fresh parsley

Cook's Tip
A variation on this soup can be made with the same quantity of dried saffron milk caps or half the quantity of dried morel mushrooms.

1 Melt the butter in a large saucepan, add the onions and brown lightly. Add the garlic, ceps and wine. Add the stock, potatoes and thyme. Simmer gently for 45 minutes.

2 Purée the soup in just a few short bursts so that pieces of mushroom are left intact. Season with lemon juice and salt and pepper.

3 To make the croutons, cut the bread into 1 in fingers. Melt the butter in a large frying pan, toss in the fingers of bread and fry until golden. Add the parsley and combine. Ladle the soup into warmed soup bowls, sprinkle with parsley croutons and serve.

Tortellini Chanterelle Broth

The savory-sweet quality of chanterelle mushrooms combines well in a simple broth with spinach-and-ricotta-filled tortellini. Serve as a starter or light main course.

SERVES 4

12 oz fresh spinach and ricotta tortellini, or 6 oz dried
5 cups chicken broth
5 tbsp dry sherry
6 oz / 1¾ cups fresh chanterelle mushrooms, trimmed and sliced, or ½ oz / ¼ cup dried
chopped fresh parsley, to garnish

1 Cook the tortellini according to the package instructions.

2 Bring the chicken broth to a boil, add the sherry and mushrooms and simmer for 10 minutes.

3 Strain the tortellini, add to the stock, ladle into four warmed soup bowls and garnish with the chopped parsley.

Cook's Tip
For a lighter version, replace the tortellini with 2 cups dried vermicelli pasta.

Champignons de Paris à la Grècque

Cultivated mushrooms are often criticized by serious mushroom pickers for a lack of flavor, but the *champignon de Paris* or Cremini mushroom is an improvement on the ubiquitous button mushroom.

SERVES 4

3 tbsp olive oil
15 little white onions, peeled
½ garlic clove, crushed
1½ lb / 6 cups Cremini mushrooms or closed field mushrooms, halved or quartered if large
1¼ cups homemade or canned chicken broth, boiling
5 tbsp white wine
2 tsp black peppercorns
4 tsp coriander seeds
1 sprig thyme
1 small bay leaf
salt and freshly ground black pepper, if necessary
1 tbsp wine vinegar
15 cherry tomatoes

1 Heat the olive oil in a large nonstick frying pan. Add the onions and brown gently over a low heat. Add the garlic and the mushrooms, stir and sauté gently until the mushrooms soften and the juices begin to run. Transfer to a large saucepan.

Cook's Tip
The flavor of these mushrooms will improve if kept refrigerated for up to a week. To peel little white onions, cover with boiling water to soften their skins.

2 Add the stock, wine, peppercorns, coriander seeds, thyme and bay leaf. Cover the surface with a round of wax paper. Simmer for 15 minutes. Add the vinegar and season if required.

3 Cover the cherry tomatoes with boiling water to loosen their skins, peel and add to the onion and mushroom mixture. Allow to cool to room temperature and serve with a basket of coarse textured bread.

Salad of Fresh Ceps with a Parsley, Egg and Walnut Dressing

To capture the just picked flavor of a cep or bay bolete, consider this delicious salad enriched with an egg yolk and walnut oil dressing. Choose small ceps and bay boletes for a firm texture and a fine flavor.

SERVES 4

12 oz / 3½ cups fresh ceps or bay boletes

6 oz mixed salad leaves, to include: escarole, young spinach and frisée

salt and freshly ground black pepper

½ cup small walnut pieces, toasted

2 oz fresh Parmesan cheese

For the Dressing

2 egg yolks

½ tsp French mustard

5 tbsp peanut oil

3 tbsp walnut oil

2 tbsp lemon juice

2 tbsp chopped fresh parsley

1 pinch superfine sugar

1 Place the egg yolks in a screw top jar with the mustard, peanut and walnut oil, lemon juice, parsley and sugar. Shake well.

2 Slice the mushrooms thinly.

3 Place the mushrooms in a large salad bowl and combine with the dressing. Leave for 10–15 minutes for the flavors to mingle.

4 Wash and dry the salad leaves, then toss with the mushrooms.

5 Turn out onto four large plates, season well, then scatter with toasted walnuts and shavings of Parmesan cheese.

Cook's Tip

For special occasions, 2–3 drops of truffle oil will impart a deep and mysterious flavor of the forests.

Cook's Tip

Be sure to use only the freshest eggs from a reputable supplier. Expectant mothers, young children and the elderly are advised not to eat raw egg yolks. If this presents a problem, the dressing can be made without the egg yolks, or with yolks cooked for 3–4 minutes.

Shaggy Ink Cap and Parasol Mushroom Soup

The shaggy ink cap forms the basis of this creamy soup and the parasol mushrooms provide additional flavor.

SERVES 4

4 tbsp unsalted butter
4 shallots or 1 medium onion, chopped
8 oz / 2½ cups shaggy ink caps, closed specimens, trimmed and chopped
1 garlic clove, crushed
3¾ cups homemade or canned chicken stock, boiling
6 oz / 1¾ cups parasol mushrooms, caps and young stems, trimmed and sliced
4 tbsp heavy cream
2 tbsp lemon juice
salt and freshly ground black pepper
3 tbsp chopped fresh parsley

1 Melt half of the butter in a saucepan, add the shallots or onion and soften over a low heat.

2 Add the ink caps and garlic and sauté gently until the mushrooms soften and the juices begin to run.

3 Add the chicken stock, bring back to a boil and simmer for 15 minutes. Purée and return to the saucepan.

4 Melt the remaining butter in a nonstick frying pan, add the parasol mushrooms and fry to soften without letting them color. Add to the saucepan and simmer for a minute.

5 Stir in the cream, add lemon juice and salt and pepper to taste. Ladle into four warmed soup bowls, sprinkle with parsley and serve with torn fresh bread.

Cook's Tip

For best results, use closed ink caps that haven't started to blacken. Once they have begun to blacken they are quite safe to eat, but they will darken the color of the soup.

An Artichoke Lover's Feast

Artichokes are a rich earthy vegetable which make a wonderful starter stuffed to the brim with a variety of cultivated and woodland mushrooms.

SERVES 4

4 large globe artichokes
1 lemon, sliced
2 tbsp butter
2 shallots or 1 small onion, chopped
8 oz / 2½ cups assorted wild and cultivated mushrooms such as ceps, bay boletes, chanterelles, saffron milk-caps, oyster mushrooms, honey, shiitake and closed field mushrooms, trimmed and chopped
1 tbsp chopped fresh thyme
For the Hollandaise Sauce
¾ cup unsalted butter
2 egg yolks
juice of ½ lemon
salt and freshly ground black pepper

1 Bring a large saucepan of salted water to a boil. With a serrated knife remove one third from the top of each artichoke. Pull off the outer leaves and discard. Break off the artichoke stems at the base, then trim about ¼ in from the base. To keep the artichokes from darkening rub the base with a slice of lemon. Place in the boiling water and cook for 25 minutes.

2 To make the mushroom filling, sauté the shallots gently in butter to soften without letting them color. Add the mushrooms and thyme, cover and cook until the juices begin to run. Increase the heat and allow the juices to evaporate. Keep warm.

3 When the artichokes are cooked (a small knife inserted in the base will indicate whether it is tender) drain and cool under running water. Remove the lemon slices and drain the artichokes upside down. To create a central cavity, pull out the small leaves from the middle of each artichoke, then scrape out the fibrous choke.

4 To make the sauce, melt the butter, skimming off any surface scum. Pour into a pitcher, leaving behind the milky residue. Place the egg yolks in a glass bowl over a saucepan of 1 in simmering water. Add ½ tsp water to the egg yolks and whisk until thick and foamy. Remove from the heat, then add the butter in a thin stream, whisking all the time. Add the lemon juice and a little boiling water to thin the sauce. Season to taste.

5 Combine one third of the sauce with the mushroom mixture and fill each of the artichokes. Serve at room temperature with the extra sauce.

Spinach with Wild Mushroom Soufflé

Wild mushrooms combine especially well with eggs and spinach in this sensational soufflé. Almost any combination of mushrooms can be used for this recipe although the firmer varieties provide the best texture.

SERVES 4

8 oz fresh spinach, washed, or 4 oz frozen chopped spinach
4 tbsp unsalted butter, plus extra for greasing
1 garlic clove, crushed
6 oz / 1¾ cups assorted wild mushrooms such as ceps, bay boletes, saffron milk-caps, oyster, field mushrooms and hen of the woods
1 cup milk
3 tbsp all-purpose flour
6 eggs, separated
salt and freshly ground black pepper
pinch grated nutmeg
2 cup freshly grated Parmesan cheese

1 Preheat the oven to 375°F. Steam the spinach over a moderate heat for 3–4 minutes. Cool under running water, then drain. Press out as much liquid as you can with the back of a large spoon and chop finely. If using frozen spinach, defrost and squeeze dry in the same way.

2 Gently sauté the garlic and mushrooms in butter. Turn up the heat and evaporate the juices. When dry, add the spinach and transfer to a bowl. Cover and keep warm.

Cook's Tip

The soufflé base can be prepared up to 12 hours in advance and reheated before the beaten egg whites are folded in.

3 Measure 3 tbsp of the milk into a bowl. Bring the remainder to a boil. Stir the flour and egg yolks into the milk in the bowl and blend well. Stir the boiling milk into the egg and flour mixture, return to the pan and simmer to thicken. Add the spinach mixture. Season to taste with salt, pepper and nutmeg.

4 Butter a 3¾ cups soufflé dish, paying special attention to the sides. Sprinkle with a little of the cheese. Set aside.

5 Whisk the egg whites until they hold soft peaks. Bring the spinach mixture back to a boil. Stir in a spoonful of beaten egg white, then fold the mixture into the remaining egg white. Turn into the soufflé dish, spread level, sprinkle with the remaining cheese and bake in the oven for about 25 minutes until puffed, risen and golden.

Alsatian Tart

Alsace is renowned for its abundance of wild mushrooms. This tart is good with a cool Alsatian wine.

SERVES 4

12 oz unsweetened pie pastry, thawed if frozen
4 tbsp unsalted butter
3 medium onions, halved and sliced
12 oz / 3½ cups assorted wild mushrooms such as ceps, bay boletes, morels, chanterelles, saffron milk-caps, oyster, field and honey mushrooms
leaves of 1 sprig thyme, chopped
salt and freshly ground black pepper
pinch of grated nutmeg
3½ tbsp whole milk
3½ tbsp light cream
1 egg and 2 egg yolks

1 Preheat the oven to 375°F and lightly grease a 9 in loose-bottomed cake or quiche pan with butter. Roll out the pastry on a lightly floured board and line the pan. Rest the pastry in the fridge for 1 hour.

Cook's Tip
To prepare ahead, the crust can be partially baked and the filling made in advance. Continue from step 3.

2 Place three squares of wax paper in the tart crust, fill with rice and bake for 25 minutes. Lift out the paper and rice and leave to cool.

3 Melt the butter in a frying pan, add the onions, cover and cook slowly for 20 minutes. Add the mushrooms and thyme, and continue cooking for another 10 minutes. Season with salt, pepper and nutmeg.

4 Place the milk and cream in a bowl and beat in the egg and egg yolks. Place the mushroom mixture in the crust and then pour over the milk and egg mixture. Bake for 15–20 minutes until the center is firm to the touch.

Stuffed Garlic Mushrooms with Prosciutto and Herbs

SERVES 4

1 medium onion, chopped
6 tbsp unsalted butter
8 medium field mushrooms
½ oz / ¼ cup dried ceps, bay boletes or saffron milk-caps, soaked in warm water for 20 minutes
1 garlic clove, crushed
¾ cup fresh bread crumbs
1 egg
5 tbsp chopped fresh parsley
1 tbsp chopped fresh thyme
salt and freshly ground black pepper
4 oz prosciutto di Parma or San Daniele, thinly sliced
fresh parsley, to garnish

1 Preheat the oven to 375 °F. Sauté the onion gently in half the butter for 6–8 minutes until soft but not colored. Meanwhile, break off the stems of the field mushrooms, setting the caps aside. Drain the dried mushrooms and chop these and the stems of the field mushrooms finely. Add to the onion together with the garlic and cook for another 2–3 minutes.

Cook's Tip
Garlic mushrooms can be easily prepared in advance ready to go into the oven.

2 Transfer the mixture to a bowl, add the bread crumbs, egg, herbs and seasoning. Melt the remaining butter in a small pan and generously brush over the mushroom caps. Arrange the mushrooms on a baking sheet and spoon in the filling. Bake in the oven for 20–25 minutes until well browned.

3 Top each with a strip of prosciutto, garnish with parsley and serve.

Mushroom Salad with Parma Ham

SERVES 4

3 tbsp unsalted butter
1 lb / 4½ cups assorted wild and cultivated mushrooms such as chanterelles, ceps, bay boletes, honey mushrooms, oyster, field and Cremini mushrooms, trimmed and sliced
4 tbsp Madeira or sherry
juice of ½ lemon
½ head of oak leaf lettuce
½ head of frisée lettuce
2 tbsp walnut oil

For the Pancake Ribbons

3 tbsp all-purpose flour
5 tbsp milk
1 egg
4 tbsp freshly grated Parmesan cheese
4 tbsp chopped fresh herbs such as parsley, thyme, marjoram or chives
salt and freshly ground black pepper
6 oz Parma ham, thickly sliced

1 To make the pancakes, blend the flour and the milk. Beat in the egg, cheese, herbs and seasoning. Pour enough of the mixture into a frying pan to coat the bottom. When the batter has set, turn the pancake over and cook briefly on the other side.

2 Turn out and cool. Roll up the pancake and slice thinly to make ½ in ribbons. Cook and cut the remaining batter in the same way and cut the ham into similar sized ribbons. Toss with the pancake ribbons.

3 Gently sauté the mushrooms in the remaining butter for 6–8 minutes until the moisture has evaporated. Add the Madeira and lemon juice, and season to taste.

4 Toss the salad leaves in the oil and arrange on four plates. Place the ham and pancake ribbons in the center, spoon on the mushrooms and serve.

Woodland Salsa Dip

This is good with mushrooms that become very soft in cooking. Firmer-fleshed mushrooms can be added to provide texture and flavor.

SERVES 4
5 tbsp olive oil
1 medium onion, chopped
1 garlic clove, crushed
1 lb eggplant, chopped
12 oz / 3½ cups shaggy ink caps, puffballs and slippery jacks, trimmed and chopped
3 oz / 1 cup chanterelles, charcoal burners, or saffron milk-caps, trimmed and chopped
3 tbsp chopped fresh parsley, chervil and chives
1 tbsp balsamic vinegar
salt and freshly ground black pepper
For Dipping
sesame bread sticks, celery, carrot, baby corn, strips of toasted pita bread

1 Heat 1 tbsp of the olive oil in a heavy saucepan over a moderate heat, add the onion and cook gently to soften without coloring.

2 Stir in the remaining oil, the garlic and eggplant, then cover and cook for 10 minutes. Add the mushrooms and cook uncovered for a further 15 minutes.

3 Stir in the herbs and vinegar and season to taste. Allow to cool and serve with bread sticks, pita bread and raw vegetables.

Cook's Tip
Woodland salsa dip will keep in the fridge in a covered container for 10 days. Do not freeze it.

Spinach and Wild Mushroom Soup

SERVES 4
2 tbsp unsalted butter
1 medium onion, chopped
12 oz / 3½ cups assorted wild and cultivated mushrooms such as ceps, bay boletes, queen bolete, shaggy ink caps, field, oyster and shiitake mushrooms, trimmed and chopped
1 garlic clove, crushed
2 tsp chopped fresh thyme or dill or 1 tsp dried
5 cups boiling homemade or canned chicken or vegetable broth
3 oz floury potato, finely chopped
14 oz fresh spinach, trimmed, or 7 oz frozen chopped spinach, defrosted and drained
salt and freshly ground black pepper
pinch of grated nutmeg
4 tbsp heavy or sour cream, to serve

Cook's Tip
If fresh wild mushrooms are unavailable, use 8 oz / 2½ cups cultivated field mushrooms with ½ oz / ¼ cup dried ceps, bay boletes or saffron milk caps.

1 Melt the butter in a large pan, add the onion and sauté gently without coloring for 6–8 minutes. Add the mushrooms, garlic and herbs, cover and allow the juices to run.

2 Add half of the broth, the potato and spinach. Bring back to a boil and simmer for 10 minutes.

3 Purée the soup and return to the saucepan. Add the remaining stock and season to taste with salt, pepper and a little nutmeg. Serve with a dollop of cream stirred into the soup.

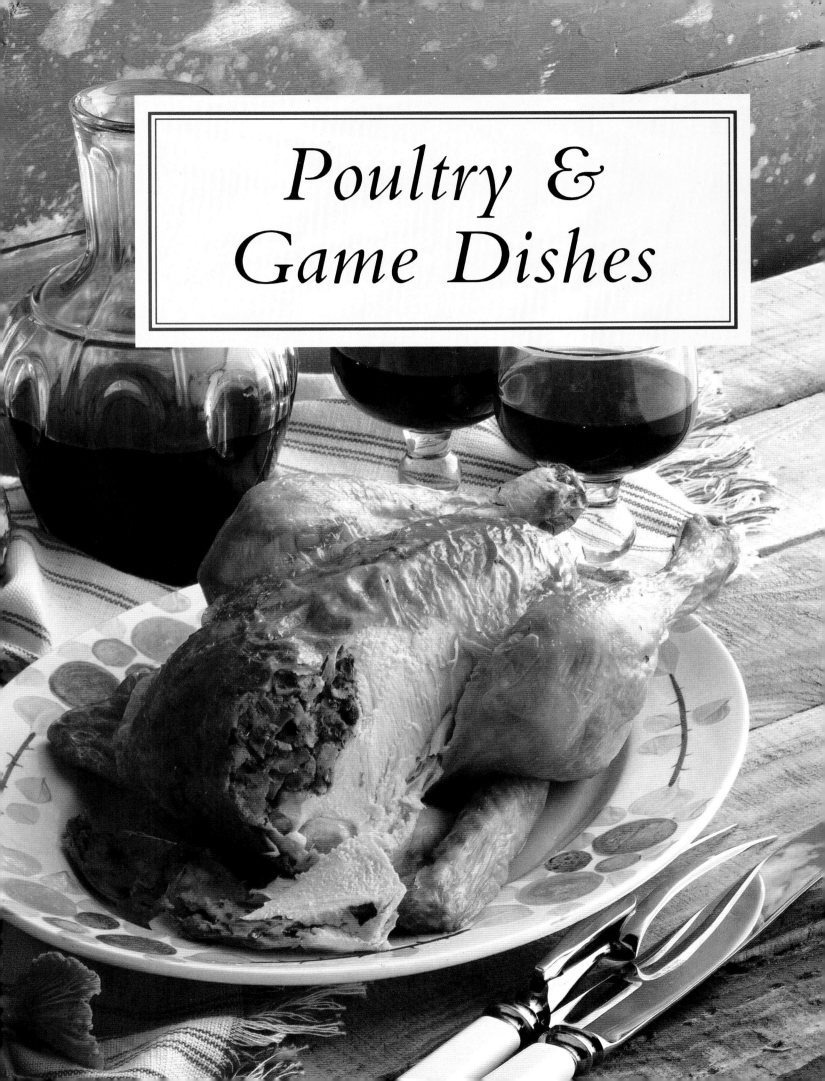

Poultry &
Game Dishes

Mushroom Picker's Chicken Paella

A good paella is based on a few well chosen ingredients. Here, wild mushrooms combine with chicken and vegetables.

SERVES 4

3 tbsp olive oil
1 medium onion, chopped
1 small bulb fennel, sliced
8 oz / 2½ cups assorted wild and cultivated mushrooms such as ceps, bay boletes, chanterelles, saffron milk-caps, hedgehog fungus, matsutake, honey and oyster mushrooms, trimmed and sliced
1 garlic clove, crushed
3 free range chicken legs, chopped through the bone
1⅔ cups short-grain Spanish or Italian rice
3¾ cups homemade or canned chicken broth, boiling
1 pinch saffron strands or 1 individual tube of saffron powder
1 sprig thyme
14 oz can wax beans, drained
¾ cup frozen peas

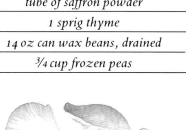

Cook's Tip
For a vegetarian mushroom paella, omit the chicken, replace the chicken broth with vegetable broth and if you can, include chicken of the woods in your choice of mushrooms.

1 Heat the olive oil in a 14 in paella pan or a large frying pan. Add the onion and fennel and sauté over a low heat for 3–4 minutes.

2 Add the mushrooms and garlic, and cook until the juices begin to run, then increase the heat to evaporate the juices. Push the onion and mushrooms to one side. Add the chicken pieces and sauté briefly.

3 Stir in the rice, add the broth, saffron, thyme, wax beans and peas. Bring to a simmer and then cook gently for 15 minutes without stirring.

4 Remove from the heat and cover the surface of the paella with a circle of greased wax paper. Cover the paper with a clean dish towel and allow the paella to finish cooking in its own heat for about 5 minutes. Bring to the table, uncover and serve.

"Chicken" of the Woods Polenta with a Cauliflower Fungus Cream

This dish contains no chicken at all and will please both meat eaters and vegetarians alike. So convincing is the flavor and texture of chicken of the woods, that many people will find it difficult to believe that they're not actually eating chicken.

SERVES 4

1 lb small new potatoes
5 1/2 cups homemade or canned light vegetable stock, boiling
6 oz young carrots, trimmed and peeled
6 oz sugar snap peas
4 tbsp unsalted butter
3 oz / 1 cup honey mushrooms or hedgehog fungus, trimmed and sliced
5 horn of plenty, fresh or dried, chopped
1 1/2 cups quick-cooking fine polenta or cornmeal
2 shallots or 1 small onion, chopped
2 fist-sized pieces cauliflower fungus or 1/2 oz / 1/4 cup dried
4 oz / 1 1/4 cups chicken of the woods, trimmed and sliced
2/3 cup light cream
3 egg yolks
2 tsp lemon juice
celery salt and cayenne pepper

Cook's Tip
If preparing this recipe in advance, make the polenta loaf and mushroom and vegetable sauce, then allow to cool. When ready to serve, reheat the polenta and sauce, then thicken the sauce with egg yolks, season and serve.

1 Lightly oil a 9 in loaf pan and line with a single sheet of wax paper. Set aside. Cover the potatoes with boiling water, add a pinch of salt and cook for 20 minutes. Bring the vegetable broth to a boil, add the carrots and peas and cook for 3–4 minutes. Remove with a slotted spoon and keep warm.

2 Add 2 tbsp of the butter and the honey mushrooms or hedgehog fungus and horn of plenty to the broth and simmer for 5 minutes. Pour in the polenta in a steady stream and stir for 2–3 minutes until thickened. Turn the polenta into the prepared pan, cover and set aside to become firm.

3 To make the sauce, melt the remaining butter, add the shallots or onion and cook gently without coloring. Add the cauliflower fungus cut into thumb-sized pieces, with the chicken of the woods, and cook for 2–3 minutes. Add the cream and the reserved cooked vegetables and simmer to evaporate excess moisture.

4 Remove from the heat, stir in the egg yolks and allow residual heat to slightly thicken the sauce. The sauce must not boil at this stage. Add the lemon juice, then season with celery salt and a dash of cayenne pepper.

5 To serve, turn the warm polenta out onto a board, slice with a wet knife and arrange on four serving plates. Spoon the mushroom and vegetable sauce over the polenta and serve with the buttered new potatoes.

Matsutake Chicken Pot Pie

Matsutake is a kingly mushroom most often found in the West. It provides a mild taste and aroma to this trans-Atlantic pot pie. It is perhaps best mixed with bay boletes, saffron milk-caps, parasol mushroom, oyster or closed field mushrooms.

SERVES 4

4 tbsp vegetable oil
1 medium onion, chopped
1 celery stalk, sliced
1 small carrot, peeled and cut into julienne strips
2 small chicken breasts, skin and bone removed
1 lb / 4½ cups matsutake mushrooms and a selection of others mentioned above, trimmed and sliced
6 tbsp all-purpose flour
2¼ cups chicken broth, boiling
2 tsp Dijon mustard
2 tbsp medium sherry
2 tsp wine vinegar
salt and freshly ground black pepper

For the Pot pie Topping

2½ cups self-rising flour
pinch of celery salt
pinch of cayenne pepper
½ cup cold unsalted butter, diced
½ cup Cheddar cheese, grated
⅔ cup cold water
1 beaten egg, to glaze, optional

1 Preheat the oven to 400°F. Heat the oil in a large heavy saucepan, add the onion, celery and carrot and sauté gently without coloring, to soften. Cut the chicken breasts into bite-sized pieces, add to the vegetables and cook briefly. Add the mushrooms, sauté until the juices run, then stir in the flour.

2 Remove the pan from the heat and stir in the broth gradually so that the flour is completely absorbed. Return the pan to the heat, and simmer gently to thicken, stirring all the time. Add the mustard, sherry, vinegar and seasoning. Cover and keep warm.

Cook's Tip
This recipe can easily be made as a pie by replacing the topping with a layer of flaky or unsweetened pie pastry.

3 To make the topping, sift the flour, celery salt and cayenne pepper into a bowl or a food processor fitted with a metal blade. Add the butter and half of the cheese, then either rub the mixture together with your fingers or process until it resembles large fresh bread crumbs. Add the water and combine without overmixing.

4 Turn out onto a floured board, form into a round and flatten to about a ½ in thickness. Cut out as many 2 in shapes as you can, using a plain cutter.

5 Transfer the chicken mixture to a 5 cup deep pie dish, then overlap the pastry shapes around the edge. Brush with beaten egg, scatter with the remaining cheese and bake in the oven for 25–30 minutes until the topping is puffed and golden.

Main Course Soup of Duck, Beets and Ceps

SERVES 4

4 tbsp butter
2 medium onions, halved and sliced
2 duck legs or breasts
5 cups chicken broth
6 oz white cabbage, sliced
1½ lb raw beets, chopped
½ oz / ¼ cup dried ceps or bay boletes
1 sprig thyme·
14 oz can wax beans
2 tbsp wine vinegar
salt and freshly ground black pepper

For the Garnish

⅔ cup sour cream
2 tbsp horseradish sauce
4 tbsp chopped fresh parsley

1 Melt the butter in a heavy saucepan, add the onions and brown lightly. Add the duck, cover with broth, then add the cabbage, beets, ceps, thyme and wax beans. Cover and simmer for 1¼ hours.

2 Skim off as much fat as you can. Remove the pieces of duck, slice into thick pieces and return to the pan. Add the vinegar and season to taste.

3 Blend the sour cream with the horseradish. Ladle the soup into bowls, and add a dollop of horseradish and some parsley. Serve with rye bread.

Roly Poly Chicken and Chanterelle Pudding

SERVES 4

1 medium onion, chopped
1 celery stalk, sliced
2 tsp chopped fresh thyme
2 tbsp vegetable oil
2 chicken breasts, skinned and boned
4 oz / 1¼ cups fresh chanterelles, trimmed and sliced, or ½ oz / ¼ cup dried, soaked in warm water for 20 minutes
4 tbsp all-purpose flour
1¼ cups homemade or canned chicken broth, boiling
1 tsp Dijon mustard
2 tsp wine vinegar
salt and freshly ground black pepper

For the Roly Poly Dough

3 cups self-rising flour
½ tsp salt
⅔ cup chilled unsalted butter, diced
5 tbsp cold water

1 Sauté the onion, celery and thyme gently in oil without coloring. Cut the chicken into bite-sized pieces, add to the pan with the mushrooms and cook briefly. Stir in the flour, then remove from the heat.

2 Stir in the chicken broth gradually so that the flour is completely absorbed by the broth. Return to the heat, simmer to thicken, then add the mustard, vinegar and seasoning. Set aside to cool.

3 To make the dough, sift the flour and salt into a bowl. Add the butter, then rub together with the fingers until it resembles coarse bread crumbs. Add the water all at once and combine without overmixing. Roll out the dough on a floured surface into a rectangle 10 × 12 in. Rinse a piece of cheesecloth, about twice as big as the dough, in a little water. Place the dough on the cheesecloth. Spread the cool chicken filling over the dough and roll up from the short end, using the cheesecloth to help, to make a fat sausage. Enclose in cheesecloth and tie each end with string.

4 Lower the pudding into a pan of boiling water, cover and simmer for 1½ hours. Lift out, untie, slice and serve.

Wild Rabbit and Mushroom Stew

The rich flavor of wild rabbit echoes the qualities of wild mushrooms.

SERVES 4

3 tbsp olive oil
12 button onions, peeled
1 celery stalk, cut into julienne sticks
1 medium carrot, cut into julienne sticks
2 lb wild rabbit portions, trimmed
salt and freshly ground black pepper
2 tbsp all-purpose flour
4 oz Jerusalem artichokes, peeled and chopped
2¼ cups chicken broth, boiling
3 oz / 1 cup fresh horn of plenty, trimmed
½ oz / ¼ cup dried ceps or bay boletes
1 tbsp green olive paste
8 green olives
1 tbsp lemon juice

1 Heat the olive oil in a heavy skillet, add the onions, celery and carrots and brown lightly for 6–8 minutes. Push to one side of the pan. Season the rabbit, add to the pan and brown quickly. Stir in the flour, add the Jerusalem artichokes, then remove from the heat.

2 Add the chicken broth gradually so that the flour is absorbed.

3 Add the mushrooms and the olive paste, cover and simmer over a low heat for 1 hour. Add the green olives and lemon juice and adjust the seasoning. Serve with parsley potatoes.

Cook's Tip
Trim away as many of the small rabbit bones as you can.

Stuffed Fennel

Vegetable fennel divides into neat boat shapes. In this recipe the shapes are baked with a creamy chicken and oyster mushroom filling and served on a bed of rice.

SERVES 4

2 large bulbs fennel
3 eggs
2 tbsp butter
1 medium onion, chopped
2 chicken breasts, skinned and boned
8 oz / 2½ cups oyster mushrooms, trimmed and chopped
4 tbsp all-purpose flour
1¼ cups homemade or canned chicken broth, boiling
1 tsp Dijon mustard
2 tbsp sherry
salt and freshly ground black pepper
parsley sprigs, to garnish

1 Preheat the oven to 375 °F. Trim the base of the fennel and pull each bulb apart into four pieces (save the central part). Boil the fennel in salted water for 3–4 minutes, then drain and leave to cool. Boil the eggs for 10 minutes. Cool, peel and set aside.

2 Finely chop the central part of the fennel. Sauté the fennel and onion gently in butter for 3–4 minutes.

3 Cut the chicken into pieces and add to the pan with the mushrooms. Cook over a moderate heat for 6 minutes, stirring frequently. Add the flour and remove from the heat.

4 Gradually add the chicken broth, making sure the flour is completely absorbed by the broth. Return to the heat and simmer until thickened, stirring all the time. Chop one of the eggs into the chicken mixture, add the mustard, sherry and seasoning to taste.

5 Arrange the fennel in a baking dish. Spoon the filling into each one, cover with foil and bake for 20–25 minutes. Serve on a bed of rice, garnished with eggs and parsley.

Sherry Braised Guinea Hen with Saffron Milk-caps

SERVES 4

2 young guinea hens, trussed
salt and freshly ground black pepper
4 tbsp unsalted butter
5 tbsp dry sherry
2 medium onions, sliced
1 small carrot, peeled and chopped
½ celery stalk, chopped
8 oz / 2½ cups assorted wild mushrooms such as saffron milk-caps or chanterelles, oyster, honey, parasol and field mushrooms, trimmed and sliced
1⅞ cup homemade or canned chicken broth, boiling
1 sprig thyme
1 bay leaf
1 tbsp lemon juice

Cook's Tip
If fresh wild mushrooms are unavailable substitute with ½ oz / ¼ cup of dried saffron milk-caps or ceps, with 3 oz / 1 cup cultivated oyster or Cremini mushrooms.

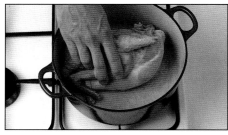

1 Preheat the oven to 375°F. Season the guinea hens with salt and pepper. Melt half of the butter in a flameproof casserole, add the birds and turn until browned all over. Transfer to a shallow dish, heat the residue in the pan, pour in the sherry and bring to a boil, stirring to deglaze the pan. Pour this liquid over the birds and set aside.

2 Wipe the casserole clean, then melt the remaining butter. Add the onions, carrots and celery. Place the birds on top, cover and cook in the oven for 40 minutes.

3 Add the chicken broth, thyme and bay leaf. Tie the mushrooms into a 12 in square of cheesecloth. Place in the casserole, cover and return to the oven for a further 40 minutes.

4 Transfer the birds to a serving platter, remove the thyme and bay leaf and set the mushrooms in the bag aside. Purée the braising liquid and pour back into the casserole. Add the mushrooms from the cheesecloth to the sauce. Season with salt and pepper and add lemon juice to taste. Heat until simmering and serve over the guinea hens or pour into a serving pitcher.

Braised Pheasant with Ceps, Chestnuts and Bacon

Pheasant at the end of their season are not suitable for roasting, so consider this delicious casserole enriched with wild mushrooms and chestnuts. Allow two birds for four people.

SERVES 4

2 mature pheasants
salt and freshly ground black pepper
4 tbsp butter
5 tbsp brandy
12 pearl onions, peeled
1 celery stalk, chopped
2 oz smoked bacon, cut into strips
3 tbsp all-purpose flour
2¼ cups homemade or canned chicken broth, boiling
6 oz peeled chestnuts
12 oz / 3½ cups fresh ceps or bay boletes, trimmed and sliced, or ½ oz / ¼ cup dried, soaked in warm water for 20 minutes
1 tbsp lemon juice
watercress sprigs, to garnish

1 Preheat the oven to 325°F. Season the pheasants with salt and pepper. Melt half of the butter in a large flameproof casserole and brown the pheasants over a moderate heat. Transfer to a shallow dish and pour off the cooking fat. Return the casserole to the heat and brown the residue. Stand back and add the brandy (the sudden flames will die down quickly). Stir to loosen the residue with a flat wooden spoon and then pour the juices over the pheasant and set aside.

2 Wipe the casserole and melt the remaining butter. Lightly brown the onions, celery and bacon. Stir in the flour. Remove from the heat.

3 Stir in the broth gradually so that it is completely absorbed by the flour. Add the chestnuts, mushrooms, the pheasants and their juices. Bring back to a gentle simmer, then cover and cook in the oven for 1½ hours.

Cook's Tip

Cooking and peeling fresh chestnuts can be hard work, so look out for canned or vacuum-packed varieties.

4 Transfer the pheasants and vegetables to a serving plate. Bring the sauce back to a boil, add the lemon juice and season to taste. Pour the sauce into a pitcher and garnish the birds.

Chicken Fricassée Forestier

The term fricassée is used to describe a light stew, usually of chicken that is first sautéed in butter. The accompanying sauce can vary, but here wild mushrooms and bacon provide a rich woodland flavor.

SERVES 4

3 free range chicken breasts, sliced
salt and freshly ground black pepper
4 tbsp unsalted butter
1 tbsp vegetable oil
4 oz smoked rindless streaky bacon, cut into pieces
5 tbsp dry sherry or white wine
1 medium onion, chopped
12 oz / 3½ cups assorted wild mushrooms such as chanterelles, ceps, bay boletes, horn of plenty, chicken of the woods, hedgehog fungus, saffron milk-caps, closed field mushrooms and cauliflower fungus, trimmed and sliced
3 tbsp all-purpose flour
2¼ cups chicken broth
2 tsp lemon juice
4 tbsp chopped fresh parsley

1 Season the chicken with pepper. Heat half of the butter and the oil in a large heavy skillet or flameproof casserole and brown the chicken and bacon pieces. Transfer to a shallow dish and pour off any excess fat.

2 Return the skillet to the heat and brown the residue. Pour in the sherry or wine and stir with a flat wooden spoon to deglaze the pan. Pour the sherry liquid over the chicken and wipe the skillet clean.

Cook's Tip
It is worth spending a little extra on properly reared free range chicken. Not only is it less fatty, but it also has a better flavor and texture.

3 Sauté the onion in the remaining butter until golden brown. Add the mushrooms and cook, stirring frequently, for 6–8 minutes, until their juices begin to run. Stir in the flour, then remove from the heat. Gradually add the chicken broth and stir well until the flour is completely absorbed.

4 Add the reserved chicken and bacon with the sherry juices, return to the heat and stir to thicken. Simmer for 10–15 minutes and then add the lemon juice, parsley and seasoning. Serve with plain boiled rice, carrots and baby corn.

Pan Fried "Chicken" of the Woods with a Sherry Cream Sauce

This dish doesn't use real chicken, the flavor, texture and aroma of *Laetiporus sulphureus* or chicken of the woods is so similar to roast chicken that it can be used in place of the real thing. There's no doubt that both vegetarians and meat eaters will enjoy this dish.

SERVES 4

4 tbsp unsalted butter
2 shallots or 1 small onion, chopped
1 celery stalk, sliced
½ medium carrot, peeled and sliced
12 oz / 3½ cups chicken of the woods, trimmed and sliced
5 tbsp all-purpose flour
1⅞ cups homemade or canned chicken or vegetable broth
5 tbsp sherry
2 tbsp chopped fresh tarragon
5 tbsp heavy cream
2 tbsp lemon juice
celery salt and cayenne pepper

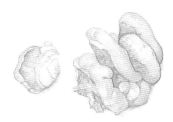

1 Melt the butter in a large skillet or flameproof casserole, add the shallots or onion, celery and carrot and sauté gently until soft but without coloring.

3 Gradually add the broth, stirring well so that the flour is absorbed. Heat gently until simmering, stirring all the time, then add the sherry and tarragon and simmer for 6–8 minutes.

2 Add the chicken of the woods, let them absorb some of the pan juices, then cook for 3–4 minutes. Stir in the flour and remove from the heat.

4 Just before serving, stir in the cream and lemon juice and season to taste with celery salt and a dash of cayenne pepper. Serve over tagliatelle or fettuccine pasta.

Cook's Tip
Instead of serving it over pasta, try this recipe as a delicious pie filling. Cover with puff or unsweetened pie pastry and bake for 45–50 minutes at 375°F.

Wild Duck Roasted with Morels and Madeira

Wild duck has a rich autumnal flavor that combines well with stronger-tasting mushrooms.

SERVES 4

2 × 2½ lb mallards, dressed and trussed weight
salt and freshly ground black pepper
4 tbsp unsalted butter
5 tbsp Madeira or sherry
1 medium onion, halved and sliced
½ celery stalk, chopped
1 small carrot, chopped
10 large dried morel mushrooms
8 oz / 2½ cups blewits, parasol and field mushrooms, trimmed and sliced
2½ cups homemade or canned chicken broth, boiling
1 sprig thyme
2 tsp wine vinegar
parsley sprigs and carrot juliennes, to garnish
roast potatoes, to serve

1 Preheat the oven to 375°F and season the ducks with salt and pepper. Melt half of the butter in a heavy skillet and brown the birds evenly. Transfer to a shallow dish, heat the residue in the pan, pour in the Madeira or sherry and bring to a boil, stirring, to deglaze the pan. Pour this liquid over the birds and set aside.

2 Heat the remaining butter in a large flameproof casserole and add the onion, celery and carrot. Place the birds on top and cook in the oven for 40 minutes, reserving the juices.

3 Tie the mushrooms in an 18 in square piece of cheesecloth. Add the broth, pan liquid, thyme and the cheesecloth bag to the casserole. Cover and return to the oven for 40 minutes.

Cook's Tip

Mallard is the most popular wild duck, although widgeon and teal are good substitutes. A widgeon will serve two but allow one teal per person.

4 Transfer the birds to a serving platter, remove and discard the thyme and set the mushrooms aside. Purée the braising liquid and pour back into the casserole. Untie the cheesecloth bag and stir the mushrooms into the sauce. Add the vinegar, season to taste and heat through gently. Garnish the ducks with parsley and carrot. Serve with roast potatoes and the Madeira or sherry sauce.

Roast Chicken Stuffed with Forest Mushrooms

A good roast chicken is a feast of flavor and succulence. Spend a little more money on a free range bird and let its flavor mingle with the wild aroma of woodland mushrooms.

SERVES 4

2 tbsp unsalted butter, plus extra for basting and to finish gravy
1 shallot, chopped
4 oz / 1¼ cups wild mushrooms such as chanterelles, ceps, bay boletes, oyster, chicken of the woods, saffron milk-caps, and hedgehog fungus, trimmed and chopped
⅔ cup fresh white, wheat, or mixed bread crumbs
salt and freshly ground black pepper
2 egg yolks
4–4½ lb free range chicken
½ celery stalk, chopped
½ small carrot, chopped
3 oz potato, peeled and chopped
1 cup homemade or canned chicken broth, plus extra if required
2 tsp wine vinegar
parsley sprigs, to garnish

1 Preheat the oven to 425°F. Melt the butter in a saucepan and gently sauté the shallot without letting it color. Add half of the chopped mushrooms and cook for 2–3 minutes until the moisture appears. Remove from the heat, stir in the bread crumbs, seasoning and egg yolks, to bind the mixture.

2 Spoon the stuffing into the neck of the chicken, enclose and fasten the skin on the underside with a skewer.

3 Rub the chicken with some extra butter and season well. Put the celery, carrot, potato and remaining mushrooms in the bottom of a roasting pan. Place the chicken on top of the vegetables, add the chicken broth and roast in the oven for 1¼ hours.

4 Transfer the chicken to a carving board or warmed serving plate, then purée the vegetables and mushrooms. Pour the mixture back into the pan and heat gently, adjusting the consistency with chicken stock if necessary. Taste and adjust seasoning, then add the vinegar and a pat of butter and stir briskly. Pour the sauce into a serving pitcher and garnish the chicken with sprigs of parsley.

Cook's Tip
If fresh mushrooms are not available, replace with ½ oz / ¼ cup of the dried equivalent and soak for 20 minutes before using.

Roast Turkey Flavored with many kinds of Mushrooms

A roast turkey on the festive table tends to look better than it tastes. One sure way to boost its flavor and succulence is to stuff it with the season's wild mushrooms. The gravy too, can be flavored with all kinds of mushrooms.

SERVES 6–8

10 lb fresh turkey, dressed weight
butter, for basting
watercress, to garnish

For the Mushroom Stuffing

4 tbsp unsalted butter
1 medium onion, chopped
8 oz / 2½ cups wild mushrooms, such as chanterelle, ceps, bay boletes, chicken of the woods, saffron milk-caps, puffballs and honey mushrooms and hedgehog fungus, trimmed and chopped
1½ cups fresh white, wheat, or mixed bread crumbs
4 oz pork sausages, skinned
1 small fresh truffle, sliced (optional)
5 drops truffle oil (optional)
salt and freshly ground black pepper

For the Gravy

5 tbsp medium sherry
1⅔ cups chicken broth
½ oz / ¼ cup dried ceps, soaked
4 tsp cornstarch
1 tsp Dijon mustard
½ tsp wine vinegar
salt and freshly ground black pepper

1 Preheat the oven to 425°F. To make the stuffing, melt the butter in a saucepan, add the onion and sauté gently without coloring. Add the mushrooms and stir until their juices begin to flow. Remove from the heat, add the bread crumbs, sausage meat and the truffle and truffle oil if using, season and stir well to combine.

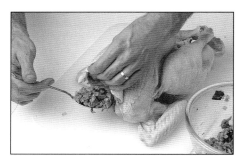

2 Spoon the stuffing into the neck cavity of the turkey and enclose, fastening the skin on the underside with a skewer.

3 Rub the skin of the turkey with butter, place in a large roasting pan and roast uncovered in the oven for 50 minutes. Lower the temperature to 350°F and cook for another 2 hours and 30 minutes.

4 To make the gravy, transfer the turkey to a carving board, cover loosely with foil and keep warm. Spoon off the fat from the roasting pan and discard. Heat the remaining liquid until reduced to a solid. Add the sherry and stir briskly with a flat wooden spoon to loosen the residue. Stir in the chicken broth.

5 Place the cornstarch and mustard in a cup, and blend with 2 tsp water and the wine vinegar. Stir this mixture into the juices in the basting pan and simmer to thicken. Season with salt and pepper and then stir in a pat of butter.

6 Garnish the turkey with bunches of watercress. Pour the gravy into a serving pitcher and serve separately.

Cook's Tip
Other sizes of turkey can be cooked this way – allow 1½ lb dressed weight of turkey per person and roast for 20 minutes per 1 lb.

Beef, Pork & Lamb

Sausage Popover with a Field Mushroom Gravy

The popover is made by pouring a simple batter over partly cooked sausages and baking in an extremely hot oven. The intense heat is essential to its lightness and volume. To accompany this feast, a dark field mushroom gravy is served straight from the pitcher.

SERVES 4

1½ lb pork sausages
1 tbsp vegetable oil
For the Batter
3 eggs
salt and freshly ground black pepper
1 cup all-purpose flour
1¼ cups whole milk
For the Mushroom Gravy
1 medium onion, chopped
2 tbsp unsalted butter
6 oz / 1¾ cups open cap field mushrooms, trimmed and sliced
1 sprig thyme, chopped
1⅞ cups homemade or canned chicken broth, boiling
1 tbsp cornstarch
1 tbsp water
1 tsp Dijon mustard

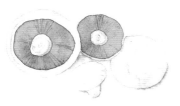

Cook's Tip
If you have time, it is a good idea to leave the batter to rest for 30–40 minutes before using. This will ensure the finished popover has a lighter texture.

1 Preheat the oven to 450°F. Prick the sausages and place them in a roasting pan with the oil. Cook in the oven for 10 minutes.

2 To make the batter, beat the eggs, season, then add the flour and stir to make a smooth paste. Add the milk a little at a time. Pour over the sausages. Bake for 35–40 minutes, until the batter is puffed and crisp.

3 To make the gravy, lightly brown the onion in butter. Add the mushrooms and thyme and sauté for 3–4 minutes until the juices begin to run. Add the stock and simmer.

4 Blend the cornstarch with the water and the mustard. Stir into the broth and simmer to thicken. Serve the popover with potatoes, broccoli, carrots and gravy.

Beef Goulash with Dark Mushrooms and Morels

A good Hungarian goulash is made rich and smooth with onions and paprika. In this recipe dark field mushrooms and morel mushrooms provide extra smoothness and a good depth of flavor.

SERVES 4

2 lb chuck steak, diced
salt and freshly ground black pepper
4 tbsp vegetable oil
⅔ cup red wine
4 medium onions, halved and sliced
1 lb / 4½ cups field or horse mushrooms or closed shaggy ink caps, trimmed and chopped
3 tbsp mild paprika
2½ cups beef broth
2 tbsp tomato paste
½ oz / ¼ cup dried morel mushrooms, soaked in warm water for 20 minutes
1 tbsp wine vinegar

1 Preheat the oven to 325°F and season the meat with pepper. Heat half of the oil in a large frying pan and fry the meat over a high heat. A quantity of liquid will appear which must be evaporated before the meat will brown and take on flavor. When the meat has browned, transfer to a flameproof casserole and pour off the fat. Return the frying pan to the heat, add the wine and stir with a flat wooden spoon to deglaze the pan. Pour the liquid over the meat and wipe the pan clean.

2 Heat the remaining oil in the pan, add the onions and brown lightly.

3 Add the mushrooms, paprika, broth, tomato paste, the morels and their liquid to the casserole. Bring to a simmer, cover and cook in the oven for about 1½ hours.

Cook's Tip
Goulash can also be made with diced pork or veal. In this case use chicken broth in place of beef. To keep the goulash a good color, select closed shaggy ink caps that have not started to blacken and deteriorate.

4 Just before serving, add the vinegar and adjust the seasoning if necessary. Serve with baked potatoes, Savoy cabbage and carrots.

Cep Meatballs with Roquefort and Walnut Sauce

The salty rich acidity of Roquefort cheese enhances the flavor of good beef. In this recipe meatballs are flavored with cep mushrooms. A Roquefort and walnut sauce makes it a dish to remember.

SERVES 4

½ oz / ¼ cup dried ceps or bay boletes, soaked in warm water for 20 minutes
1 lb lean ground beef
1 small onion, finely chopped
2 egg yolks
1 tbsp chopped fresh thyme
celery salt and freshly ground black pepper
2 tbsp olive oil

For the Roquefort Sauce
⅞ cup milk
2 oz walnuts, toasted
3 slices white bread, crusts removed
3 oz Roquefort cheese
4 tbsp chopped fresh parsley

1 Drain the mushrooms, reserving the liquid, and chop finely. Place the beef, onion, egg yolks, thyme and seasoning in a bowl, add the mushrooms and combine well. Divide the mixture into thumb-sized pieces with wet hands and roll into balls.

2 To make the sauce, place the milk in a small pan and bring to a simmer. Put the walnuts in a food processor and grind until smooth, then add the bread and pour in the milk and reserved mushroom liquid. Add the cheese and parsley, then process until smooth. Transfer to a mixing bowl, cover and keep warm.

3 Heat the olive oil in a large nonstick frying pan. Cook the meatballs in two batches for 6–8 minutes. Add the sauce to the pan and heat very gently without allowing it to boil, then turn into a serving dish or serve over ribbon pasta.

Old English Steak and Mushroom Pudding

This pudding has been lost to the fast-food lifestyle. It takes five hours to cook but it is worth waiting for!

SERVES 4

1 lb chuck steak, diced
8 oz / 2½ cups assorted wild and cultivated mushrooms such as chanterelles, ceps, queen bolete, shaggy ink caps, horn of plenty, saffron milk-caps, blewits, oyster, field and honey mushrooms and not more than 3 dried morels, trimmed and sliced
1 medium onion, chopped
3 tbsp all-purpose flour
celery salt and freshly ground black pepper
3 shakes Worcestershire sauce
½ cup beef broth

For the Pastry Crust
2 cups self-rising flour
½ tsp salt
6 tbsp cold butter, grated
⅔ cup cold water

1 To make the pastry, sift the flour and salt into a bowl and stir in the butter. Add all of the water and stir with a fork to form a loose dough. Turn out onto a floured surface and press together without overworking.

2 Brush a 5 cup pudding mold with oil or butter. Roll out the dough with a dusting of flour to form a 10 in circle. Cut out a quarter section and save for the top. Line the mold and set aside.

3 Mix the beef, mushrooms, onion, flour and seasoning in a large bowl. Transfer to the lined mold, add the Worcestershire sauce and then the beef broth. Bring overlapping pastry edges towards the center, moisten with water and cover the top with the leftover pastry.

4 Place a circle of wax paper on the pastry, then cover the whole basin with an 18 in piece of foil. Boil 2 in of water in a pan and lower the mold into the pan. Cover and steam for 2½ hours, making sure the water doesn't boil away.

5 When ready to serve, unmold onto a plate and serve with curly kale, carrots and boiled potatoes.

Rich Beef Stew with Cep Dumplings

As if the temptation of a rich beef stew isn't enough, here it is crowned with cep dumplings.

SERVES 4

4 tbsp vegetable oil
2 lb chuck steak, diced
2/3 cup red wine
2 medium onions, halved and sliced
1/2 celery stalk, chopped
lb / 4 1/2 cups open cap wild or cultivated field mushrooms, sliced
1/2 garlic clove, crushed
2 1/2 cups beef broth
2 tbsp tomato paste
2 tsp black olive paste
1 tbsp wine vinegar
1 tsp anchovy sauce
1 sprig thyme
salt and freshly ground black pepper

For the Cep Dumplings

2 1/4 cups self-rising flour
1/2 tsp salt
1/2 cup cold butter or margarine, finely diced
3 tbsp chopped fresh parsley
1 tsp chopped fresh thyme
1/2 oz / 1/4 cup dried ceps, soaked in warm water for 20 minutes
1 cup cold milk

1 Preheat the oven to 325°F. Lightly season the meat with pepper, then heat half of the oil in a pan, and seal the meat over a high heat. The liquid that appears must be evaporated before the meat will brown.

2 When the meat has browned, transfer to a flameproof casserole and pour off the fat from the pan. Add the wine to the pan and stir with a flat wooden spoon to loosen the residue. Pour over the meat.

3 Wipe the pan clean, then heat the remaining oil, add the onions and celery and brown lightly. Add to the casserole with the mushrooms, garlic, beef broth, tomato and olive paste, vinegar, anchovy sauce and thyme. Bring to a simmer, cover and cook in the oven for 1 1/2–2 hours.

4 To make the dumplings, sift the flour and salt together, add the butter, then the parsley and thyme. Drain the ceps and chop finely. Add the ceps and milk to the mixture and stir with a knife to make a soft dough, taking care not to overmix.

5 Flour your hands and form the mixture into thumb-sized dumplings. Drop them into simmering water and cook uncovered for 10–12 minutes. When cooked, remove and arrange on top of the stew.

Braised Beef with Mushroom Gravy

Delicious gravy is an integral part of a good stew.

SERVES 4

2 lb chuck steak, sliced
salt and freshly ground black pepper
4 tbsp vegetable oil
2/3 cup red wine
2 medium onions, halved and sliced
1/2 celery stalk, chopped
1 lb / 4 1/2 cups open cap wild or cultivated field mushrooms, sliced
1/2 garlic clove, crushed
2 1/2 cups beef broth
2 tbsp tomato paste
2 tsp black olive paste
1 tsp anchovy sauce
1 sprig thyme
1 tbsp wine vinegar

1 Preheat the oven to 325°F. Season the meat with pepper. Heat half of the oil in a large frying pan, and brown the beef over a high heat. Liquid will appear, which must be evaporated before the meat will brown and take on flavor.

2 Transfer the meat to a flameproof casserole and pour off the fat from the pan. Return the pan to the heat, add the wine and stir briskly. Pour over the meat and wipe the pan clean.

3 Heat the remaining oil in the pan, add the onions and celery and brown lightly. Add the mushrooms, garlic, beef broth, tomato and olive paste, anchovy sauce and thyme to the casserole. Set over the heat and bring to a simmer. Cover and cook in the oven for about 2 hours until the meat is tender. Add the vinegar and adjust the seasoning. Serve with mashed potatoes, rutabagas and cabbage.

Lamb Chop Sauté with a Sauce of Woodland Mushrooms

SERVES 4

4 × 6oz lamb chops
salt and freshly ground black pepper
2 tbsp olive oil
1/3 cup red wine
8 oz / 2 1/2 cups assorted wild and cultivated mushrooms, such as chanterelles, ceps, bay boletes, horn of plenty, saffron milk-caps, parasol mushrooms, oyster, puffballs, honey or field mushrooms, trimmed and sliced
1/2 garlic clove, crushed
7/8 cup homemade or canned chicken broth, boiling
2 tsp cornstarch
1 tsp Dijon mustard
1/2 tsp black olive paste
1 tsp wine vinegar
2 tbsp unsalted butter

1 Season the lamb with black pepper, then moisten with 1 tbsp of the oil. Sauté over a steady heat for 6–8 minutes for medium-rare meat or 12–15 minutes for well done.

Cook's Tip

Do not season cut pieces of meat with salt before cooking. This can cause the meat to dry and toughen. Season before serving.

2 Transfer the lamb to a plate, cover and keep warm. Pour off any excess oil from the pan and heat the residue until it browns. Add the red wine and stir with a flat wooden spoon to loosen the residue. Add the mushrooms, stir briefly and then add the chicken broth and simmer for 3–4 minutes.

3 Place the cornstarch, mustard and olive paste in a cup and blend with 1 tbsp cold water. Stir into the pan and simmer briefly to thicken. Add the vinegar, stir in the butter and season to taste. Season the lamb with a little salt, spoon the sauce over the top and serve with sautéed potatoes, green beans and carrots.

Black Pepper Beef Steaks with Red Wine and Mushroom Sauce

SERVES 4

4 × 8oz sirloin or rump steaks
1 tbsp black peppercorns, cracked
1 tbsp olive oil
1/2 cup red wine
8 oz / 2 1/2 cups assorted wild and cultivated mushrooms such as ceps, bay boletus, chanterelles, horn of plenty, saffron milk-caps, blewits, morels, Paris mushrooms, field, oyster, hen of the woods and honey mushrooms or cauliflower fungus, trimmed and sliced
1/2 garlic clove, crushed
1 1/4 cups beef broth
1 tbsp cornstarch
1 tsp Dijon mustard
2 tsp fish sauce (optional)
1 tsp wine vinegar
5 tbsp crème fraîche

1 Place a large frying pan over a high heat. Season the steaks with cracked pepper and moisten with oil.

Cook's Tip

In terms of both flavor and tenderness, the best cut of steak is taken from the rump end. Rib steaks are also good, but because of their size, they are best suited to serve two.

2 Fry the steaks for 6–8 minutes for medium-rare meat, or 12–15 minutes for well done, turning once. Transfer to a plate and keep warm.

3 Pour off any excess fat, return the pan to the heat and brown the residue. Add the wine and loosen the residue with a flat wooden spoon. Add the mushrooms and garlic and sauté for 6–8 minutes. Add the stock.

4 Place the cornstarch and mustard in a cup and blend with 1 tbsp cold water. Stir into the pan juices and simmer to thicken. Add the fish sauce, if using, the vinegar, and the crème fraîche. Spoon the sauce over the steaks and sprinkle with parsley.

Beef Stroganoff with a Chanterelle Parsley Cream

This dish is believed to be named after a 19th-century Russian diplomat, Count Paul Stroganoff. It was originally made with fillet steak, wild mushrooms and cream, but has suffered many changes. Here is an attempt at the original.

SERVES 4

1 lb fillet or rump steak, trimmed and cut into thin strips
salt and freshly ground black pepper
2 tbsp olive oil
3 tbsp brandy
2 shallots, finely chopped
8 oz / 2½ cups chanterelle mushrooms, trimmed and halved
⅔ cup beef stock
5 tbsp sour cream
1 tsp Dijon mustard
½ sweet gherkin, chopped
3 tbsp chopped fresh parsley

1 Season the steak with pepper, heat half of the oil in a pan and cook for 2 minutes. Transfer the meat to a plate.

Cook's Tip
If you can't afford fillet steak, buy best rump or sirloin.

2 Place the pan over a moderately high heat and brown the sediment. Stand back from the pan, add the brandy, tilt towards the flame (or ignite with a match if cooking on an electric hob) and burn off the liquor vapor. Pour these juices over the meat, cover and keep warm.

3 Wipe the pan clean, heat the remaining oil and lightly brown the shallots. Add the mushrooms and fry gently for 3–4 minutes to soften.

4 Add the stock and simmer for a few minutes and then add the sour cream, mustard and gherkin together with the steak and its juices. Simmer briefly, season to taste and stir in the chopped parsley. Serve with buttered noodles dressed with poppy seeds.

Sauté of Pork with Jerusalem Artichokes and Horn of Plenty

The Jerusalem artichoke has an earthy quality not unlike the flavors of the horn of plenty.

SERVES 4

3 tbsp vegetable oil
1 medium onion, halved and sliced
1 celery stick, sliced
1 medium carrot, peeled, halved and sliced
1½ lb lean pork, loin or thick end, cut into strips
3 tbsp all-purpose flour
2¼ cups chicken stock
3 oz Jerusalem artichokes, peeled and thickly sliced
4 oz / 1¼ cups horn of plenty or winter chanterelles, trimmed
1 tbsp green olive paste
1 tbsp lemon juice
salt and freshly ground black pepper

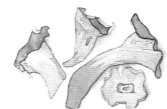

Cook's Tip
Jerusalem artichokes go a long way to provide richness to a dish. If used in excess, however, they sometimes cause flatulence.

1 Heat the oil in a heavy skillet or frying pan, add the onion, celery and carrot and fry gently for 6–8 minutes to soften.

2 Push the vegetables to one side of the pan, add the pork and seal. Stir in the flour and remove from the heat.

3 Add the stock gradually and stir so that the flour is completely absorbed by the stock.

4 Add the artichokes, mushrooms and olive paste and bring to a simmer. Cover with a lid or foil and cook very gently for about 1 hour. Add the lemon juice, adjust the seasoning and serve with a mixture of wild and long grain rice and petits pois.

Pork Sausage Puff with a Filling of Wild Mushrooms

Fresh pork sausages needn't be cooked in their casing. To make the most of them, remove the meat and wrap it in a puff pastry package. A thick seam of wild mushrooms gives a seasonal twist.

SERVES 4

4 tbsp unsalted butter
½ garlic clove, crushed
1 tbsp chopped fresh thyme
1 lb / 4½ cups assorted wild and cultivated mushrooms such as ceps, bay boletes, chanterelles, horn of plenty, saffron milk-caps, blewits, chicken of the woods, oyster, field, hen of the woods and honey mushrooms, trimmed and sliced
1 cup fresh white bread crumbs
5 tbsp chopped fresh parsley
salt and freshly ground black pepper
12 oz puff pastry, thawed if frozen
1½ lb best pork sausages
1 egg, beaten with a pinch of salt

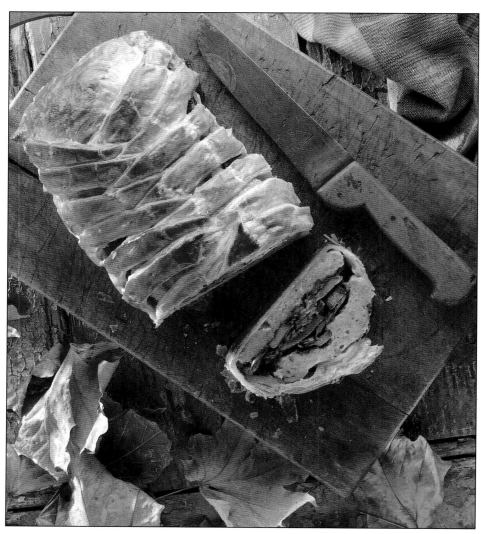

1 Preheat the oven to 350°F. Melt the butter in a large non-stick frying pan, add the garlic, thyme and mushrooms and sauté gently for 5–6 minutes. When the mushroom juices begin to run, increase the heat to evaporate the juices. When dry, stir in the bread crumbs and chopped parsley and season well.

2 Roll out the pastry on a floured surface to form a 14 × 10 in rectangle and place on a large ungreased baking sheet.

3 Immerse the sausages in a bowl of water, pierce and pull off their casings. Place half of the sausage meat in a 5 in strip along the center of the pastry. Cover with mushrooms, then with another layer of sausage meat.

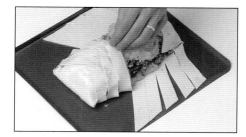

4 Make a series of 1 in slanting cuts in the pastry each side of the filling. Fold the two ends of pastry over the filling, moisten the pastry with beaten egg and then cross the top with alternate strips of pastry from each side. Allow to rest for 40 minutes, brush with a little more egg and bake in the oven for 1 hour.

Cook's Tip
A good pinch of salt added to a beaten egg will melt down and improve the finished glaze.

Coriander Lamb Kebabs with Almond Chanterelle Sauce

The delicate sweetness of lamb combines well with apricot-scented chanterelles, used here to make this especially delicious almond sauce.

SERVES 4

8 lamb cutlets, trimmed
2 tbsp unsalted butter
8 oz / 2½ cups chanterelle mushrooms, trimmed
¼ cup whole almonds, toasted
2 oz white bread, crusts removed
1 cup milk
3 tbsp olive oil
½ tsp superfine sugar
2 tsp lemon juice
salt and cayenne pepper

For the Marinade

3 tbsp olive oil
1 tbsp lemon juice
2 tsp ground cilantro
½ garlic clove, crushed
2 tsp honey

1 Mix all marinade ingredients together, pour over the lamb and leave for at least 30 minutes.

2 Fry the chanterelles gently in butter without coloring for 3–4 minutes. Set aside.

3 Place the almonds in a processor and grind finely. Add half of the chanterelles, the bread, milk, oil, sugar and lemon juice, then process.

4 Preheat a moderate broiler. Thread the lamb onto four metal skewers, and broil for 6–8 minutes on each side. Season the sauce, then spoon over the kebobs. Add the remaining chanterelles and serve with potatoes and a salad.

Cook's Tip
Almond chanterelle sauce makes a delicious dressing for pasta. Serve with a handful of chanterelles cooked in butter.

Beef Wellington Enriched with Mushrooms

There are two ways of preparing beef Wellington: both involve a length of beef tenderloin wrapped and baked in flaky pastry. Traditionally the beef is spread with a layer of goose liver pâté, but because of its high price, many cooks turn to an equally delicious and infinitely cheaper pâté of woodland mushrooms.

SERVES 4

1½ lb beef tenderloin, tied
freshly ground black pepper
1 tbsp vegetable oil
12 oz puff pastry, thawed if frozen
1 egg, beaten, to glaze

For the Parsley Pancakes

5 tbsp all-purpose flour
a pinch of salt
⅔ cup milk
1 egg
2 tbsp chopped fresh parsley

For the Mushroom Pâté

2 tbsp unsalted butter
2 shallots or 1 small onion, chopped
1 lb / 4½ cups assorted wild and cultivated mushrooms such as oyster mushrooms, ceps, bay boletes, queen bolete, shaggy ink caps, chanterelles, saffron milk caps, parasol mushrooms, blewits, closed field or honey mushrooms, trimmed and chopped
1 cup fresh white bread crumbs
8 tbsp heavy cream
2 egg yolks

1 Preheat the oven to 425°F. Season the beef with several twists of black pepper. Heat the oil in a roasting pan, add the beef and quickly sear to brown all sides. Transfer to the oven and roast for 15 minutes for rare, 20 minutes for medium-rare or 25 minutes for well done meat. Set aside to cool. Reduce the temperature to 375°F.

2 To make the pancakes, beat the flour, salt, half the milk, the egg and parsley together until smooth, then stir in the remaining milk. Heat a greased, nonstick pan and pour in enough batter to coat the bottom. When set, turn over and cook the other side briefly until lightly browned. Continue with remaining batter – the recipe makes three or four.

3 To make the mushroom pâté, sauté the shallots or onion in butter to soften without coloring. Add the mushrooms and cook until their juices begin to run. Increase the heat and cook briskly so that the juices evaporate. Combine the bread crumbs with the cream and egg yolks. When the mushrooms are dry, add the bread and cream mixture and blend to make a smooth paste. Allow to cool.

Cook's Tip

Beef Wellington can be prepared up to 8 hours in advance but should be kept at room temperature as the meat will not heat through in the cooking times given if it is chilled before cooking begins. Instead of using a meat thermometer, you can insert a metal skewer into the meat. If the skewer is cold the meat is not done, if it is warm the meat is rare and if it is hot it is well-done.

4 Roll out the pastry and cut into a rectangle 14 × 12 in. Place two pancakes on the pastry and spread with mushroom pâté. Place the beef on top and spread over any remaining pâté. Cover with the remaining pancakes. Cut out four squares from the corners of the pastry. Moisten the pastry edges with egg and then wrap them over the meat.

5 Decorate the top with the reserved pastry trimmings, transfer to a baking sheet and rest in a cool place until ready to cook.

6 Brush evenly with beaten egg. Cook the Wellington for about 40 minutes until golden brown. To ensure that the meat is heated through, test with a meat thermometer. It should read 125–130°F for rare, 135–140°F for medium-rare and 155–160°F for well-done meat.

Roast Leg of Lamb with a Wild Mushroom Stuffing

When the thigh bone is removed from a leg of lamb, a stuffing can be put in its place. This not only makes the lamb easier to carve but also gives an excellent flavor to the meat.

SERVES 4

4 lb leg of lamb, boned

salt and freshly ground black pepper

For the Wild Mushroom Stuffing

2 tbsp butter, plus extra if needed for gravy

1 shallot or 1 small onion

8 oz / 2½ cups assorted wild and cultivated mushrooms such as chanterelles, ceps, bay boletes, horn of plenty, blewits, oyster, puffballs, field and honey mushrooms, trimmed and chopped

½ garlic clove, crushed

1 sprig thyme, chopped

1 oz crustless white bread, diced

2 egg yolks

salt and freshly ground black pepper

For the Wild Mushroom Gravy

3½ tbsp red wine

1⅔ cups chicken broth, boiling

⅙ oz / 2 tbsp dried ceps, bay boletes or saffron milk-caps, soaked in boiling water for 20 minutes

4 tsp cornstarch

1 tsp Dijon mustard

½ tsp wine vinegar

a pat of butter

watercress, to garnish

1 Preheat the oven to 400°F. To make the stuffing, melt the butter in a large nonstick frying pan and gently fry the shallot or onion without coloring. Add the mushrooms, garlic and thyme and stir until the mushrooms juices begin to run, then increase the heat so that they evaporate completely.

2 Transfer the mushrooms to a mixing bowl, add the bread, egg yolks and seasoning and mix well. Allow to cool slightly.

3 Season the inside cavity of the lamb and then press the stuffing into the cavity, using a spoon or your fingers. Tie up the end with fine string and then tie around the lamb so that it does not lose its shape.

4 Place the lamb in a roasting pan and roast in the oven for 15 minutes per 1 lb for rare meat and 20 minutes per 1 lb for medium-rare. A 4 lb leg will take 1 hour 20 minutes if cooked medium-rare.

5 Transfer the lamb to a warmed serving plate, cover and keep warm. To make the gravy, spoon off all excess fat from the roasting tin and brown the residue over a moderate heat. Add the wine and stir with a flat wooden spoon to loosen the residue. Add the chicken broth, the mushrooms and their soaking liquid.

6 Place the cornstarch and mustard in a cup and blend with 1 tbsp water. Stir into the broth and simmer to thicken. Add the vinegar. Season to taste, and stir in the butter. Garnish the lamb with watercress, and serve with roast potatoes, carrots and broccoli.

Cook's Tip
If you buy your meat from a butcher, ask for the thigh bone to be taken out.

Fish & Shellfish

Shellfish Risotto with Fruits of the Forest

The creamy nature of short-grain rice cooked with onions and a simple stock provides the basis for this delicious combination of shellfish and mushrooms.

SERVES 4

3 tbsp olive oil
1 medium onion, chopped
8 oz / 2½ cups assorted wild and cultivated mushrooms such as ceps, bay boletus, chanterelles, chicken of the woods, saffron milk-caps, horn of plenty, wood blewits, oyster, horse mushrooms and truffles, trimmed and sliced
1 lb / 2¼ cups short-grain Arborio or other short-grained rice
5 cups homemade or canned chicken or vegetable broth, boiling
⅔ cup white wine
4 oz raw shrimp, peeled
8 oz raw mussels in their shells
8 oz littleneck clams
1 medium squid, cleaned, trimmed and sliced
3 drops truffle oil (optional)
5 tbsp chopped fresh parsley and chervil
celery salt and cayenne pepper

Cook's Tip
Before cooking, scrub the mussels and clams, then tap them with a knife. If any of the shells do not close, discard them. After cooking (see step 3), if any of the shells have not opened discard them too.

1 Heat the oil in a large skillet and sauté the onion for 6–8 minutes until soft but not brown.

3 Pour in the stock and wine. Add the shrimp, mussels, clams and squid, stir and simmer for 15 minutes.

2 Add the mushrooms and sauté until their juices begin to run. Stir in the rice and heat through.

4 Add the truffle oil if using, stir in the herbs, cover and stand for 5–10 minutes. Season to taste with celery salt and a pinch of cayenne pepper and serve with coarse-textured bread.

Deep Sea Scallops in a Forest of Wild Mushrooms

From the depths of the sea and forest come two flavors that marry perfectly in a smooth creamy sauce.

SERVES 4

12 oz puff pastry, thawed if frozen
1 egg, beaten, to glaze
6 tbsp unsalted butter
12 scallops, trimmed and thickly sliced
salt and freshly ground black pepper
2 shallots, chopped
½ celery stalk, cut into strips
½ medium carrot, peeled and cut into strips
8 oz / 2½ cups assorted wild mushrooms, such as chanterelles, chicken of the woods, cauliflower fungus, oyster, brick caps and honey mushrooms, trimmed and sliced
4 tbsp Noilly Prat or other dry white vermouth
⅔ cup crème fraîche
4 egg yolks
1 tbsp lemon juice
celery salt and cayenne pepper

1 Roll the pastry out on a floured surface, cut into four 5 in circles, and then trim into shell shapes. Brush with a little beaten egg and mark a shell pattern on each with a small knife. Place on a baking sheet, chill and rest for 1 hour. Preheat the oven to 400°F.

2 Melt 2 tbsp of the butter in a pan, season the scallops and cook for not longer than 30 seconds over a high heat. Transfer to a plate.

3 Bake the pastry shapes for 20–25 minutes until golden and dry. Sauté the shallots, celery and carrots gently in the remaining butter without coloring. Add the mushrooms and cook over a moderate heat until the juices begin to run. Pour in the vermouth and increase the heat to evaporate the juices.

4 Add the crème fraîche and cooked scallops and bring to a simmer (do not boil). Remove the pan from the heat and blend in the egg yolks. Return the pan to a gentle heat and cook for a moment or two until the sauce has thickened to the consistency of thin cream, remove the pan from the heat. Season and add the lemon juice.

5 Split the pastry shapes open and place on four plates. Spoon in the filling and replace the tops. Serve with potatoes and salad.

Cook's Tip
Take care not to use dark mushrooms in a cream sauce.

Clam, Mushroom and Potato Chowder

SERVES 4

48 medium clams, washed
1 tbsp unsalted butter
1 large onion, chopped
1 celery stalk, sliced
1 medium carrot, peeled and sliced
8 oz / 2½ cups assorted wild mushrooms such as chanterelles, saffron milk-caps, chicken of the woods or oyster mushrooms, trimmed and sliced
8 oz potatoes, peeled and thickly sliced
5 cups light chicken or vegetable broth, boiling
1 sprig thyme
3 tbsp chopped fresh parsley, plus 4 parsley stalks
salt and freshly ground black pepper

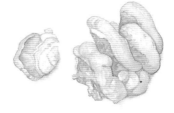

1 Place the clams in a large stainless steel pan, put ½ in of water in the bottom, cover and steam over a moderate heat for 6–8 minutes.

2 When open, drain the clams over a bowl, remove the shells and chop. Strain the juices over and set aside.

3 Add the butter, onion, celery and carrot to the pan and soften without coloring. Add the mushrooms and cook for 3–4 minutes until their juices begin to run. Add the potatoes, the clams and their juices, the broth, thyme and parsley stalks. Bring to a boil and simmer for 25 minutes, or until the potatoes begin to fall apart. Season to taste, ladle into soup plates, sprinkle with parsley and serve.

Cook's Tip
If clams are not available, use the same quantity of mussels.

Snails with Ceps

SERVES 4

12 oz puff pastry, thawed if frozen
1 egg, beaten, to glaze
½ cup grated Parmesan
4 tbsp unsalted butter
2 shallots, finely chopped
2 oz fennel, finely chopped
2 oz fine green beans, cut in three
4 oz / 1¼ cups fresh ceps, sliced, or ½ oz / ¼ cup dried ceps, soaked in warm water for 20 minutes and chopped
1 garlic clove, crushed
5 tbsp dry sherry
⅔ cup beef broth, boiling
2 tsp cornstarch
1 tsp Dijon mustard
2 × 7oz cans snails, drained
½ tsp black olive paste
1 tsp balsamic or wine vinegar
salt and freshly ground black pepper
3 tbsp chopped fresh parsley

1 Roll out the pastry on a floured surface to a 12 in square. Cut out eight 4 in fluted rings, then cut four circles with a 3 in plain cutter. Place the four circles on a baking sheet, top each with two pastry rings and brush with beaten egg.

2 Roll out the trimmings in a dusting of Parmesan cheese, cut into ¾ in wide strips and wind around four cream horn molds. Chill all the pastry shapes for about 1 hour.

3 Preheat the oven to 400°F. Melt the butter in a large nonstick frying pan, and gently fry the shallots, fennel and beans until soft but not brown. Add the ceps and garlic and sauté for another 6 minutes. Add the sherry and broth and simmer briefly. Bake the pastry shapes for 25 minutes until crisp.

4 Place the cornstarch and the mustard in a cup and blend with 1 tbsp cold water. Stir the cornstarch mixture into the pan and simmer to thicken. Add the snails and the olive paste and simmer to heat through, then add the vinegar and season to taste.

5 Spoon the mixture into the pastry shapes and sprinkle with chopped parsley. Serve with creamed potatoes and Savoy cabbage.

Fillets of Trout with a Spinach and Field Mushroom Sauce

Many people like the idea of trout, but have trouble getting it off the bone. Trout fillets are the answer to this problem and taste delicious with a rich spinach and mushroom sauce.

SERVES 4

4 brown or rainbow trout, filleted and skinned to make 8 fillets

For the Spinach and Mushroom Sauce

6 tbsp unsalted butter

¼ medium onion, chopped

8 oz / 2½ cups closed field or horse mushrooms, chopped

1¼ cups homemade or canned chicken broth, boiling

8 oz frozen chopped spinach

2 tsp cornstarch

⅔ cup crème fraîche

salt and freshly ground black pepper

grated nutmeg

1 To make the sauce, melt 4 tbsp of the butter in a frying pan and sauté the onion until soft. Add the mushrooms and cook until the juices begin to run. Add the broth and the spinach and cook until the spinach has completely thawed.

2 Blend the cornstarch with 1 tbsp of cold water and stir into the mushroom mixture. Simmer gently to thicken.

3 Purée the sauce until smooth, add the crème fraîche and season to taste with salt and pepper and a pinch of nutmeg. Turn into a serving pitcher and keep warm.

4 Melt the remaining butter in a large nonstick frying pan. Season the trout and cook for 6 minutes, turning once. Serve with new potatoes and young carrots with the sauce either poured over or served separately.

Cook's Tip
Spinach and mushroom sauce is also good with fillets of cod, haddock and sole.

Puff Pastry Salmon with Chanterelle Cream Filling

The flavor of farmed salmon is helped by a creamy layer of chanterelle mushrooms.

SERVES 6

12 oz puff pastry, thawed if frozen
1 egg, beaten, to glaze
2 large salmon fillets, about 2 lb total weight, skinned and boned
1⅝ cups dry white wine
1 small carrot
1 small onion, halved
½ celery stalk, chopped
1 sprig thyme

For the Chanterelle Cream

2 tbsp unsalted butter
2 shallots, chopped
8 oz / 2½ cups chanterelles or saffron milk-caps, trimmed and sliced
5 tbsp white wine
⅔ cup heavy cream
3 tbsp chopped fresh chervil
2 tbsp chopped fresh chives

For the Hollandaise Sauce

¾ cup unsalted butter
2 egg yolks
2 tsp lemon juice
salt and freshly ground black pepper

1 Preheat the oven to 400°F. Roll out the pastry on a floured surface to form a rectangle 4 in longer and 2 in wider than the fillets. Trim into a fish shape, decorate with a pastry cutter and glaze with beaten egg. Chill for at least 1 hour and then bake for 30–35 minutes until puffed and golden. Remove from the oven, cool slightly, and split open horizontally. Reduce the oven temperature to 325 °F.

2 To make the chanterelle cream, sauté the shallots gently in butter until soft but not colored. Add the mushrooms and cook until their juices begin to run. Pour in the wine, increase the heat and evaporate the juices. When dry, add the cream and herbs and bring to a simmer. Season well, transfer to a bowl, cover and keep warm.

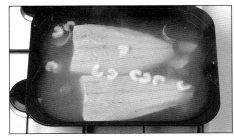

3 To poach the salmon fillets, place in a fish poacher or roasting pan. Add the wine, carrot, onion, celery, thyme and enough water to cover the fish. Bring to a boil slowly. As soon as the water begins to tremble, remove from the heat, cover and allow the fish to cook at this gentle simmer for 30 minutes.

4 To make the sauce, melt the butter, skim the surface of any scum and pour into a small pitcher, leaving behind the milky residue. Place the yolks and 1 tbsp of water in a glass bowl and place over a pan of simmering water. Whisk the yolks until thick and foamy. Remove from the heat and very slowly pour in the butter, whisking all the time. Add the lemon juice and season.

5 Place one salmon fillet on the base of the pastry, spread with the chanterelle cream and cover with the second fillet. Cover with the top of the pastry "fish" and warm through in the oven for about 10–15 minutes. Serve with the sauce.

Cook's Tip
Fillets of cod or haddock would also be good in this pastry "fish".

Wild Mushroom and Cep Cockle Puffs

This dish is as much a soup as it is a fish course. Oyster mushrooms, ceps and cockles or mussels combine in a rich herb broth and covered with pastry. When baked, the broth steams and the pastry puffs in a dome.

SERVES 4

12 oz puff pastry, thawed, if frozen
1 egg beaten, to glaze
3 tbsp sesame seeds or celery seed
For the Soup
2 tbsp unsalted butter
4 scallions, trimmed and chopped
1 celery stalk, sliced
1 small carrot, peeled, halved and sliced
4 oz / 1¼ cups fresh young ceps or bay boletes, sliced
6 oz / 1¾ cups oyster mushrooms
1⅞ cup whole milk
10 oz shelled fresh cockles or mussels, cooked
2 oz samphire or glasswort, trimmed (optional)
4 oz cooked potato, diced
4 sprigs thyme

1 Roll out the pastry on a floured surface and cut into four 7 in rounds. Rest in a cool place for 1 hour. Preheat the oven to 375°F.

2 Fry the scallions, celery and carrot in butter for 2–3 minutes. Add the mushrooms and sauté until the juices begin to flow. Transfer to a large saucepan.

3 Pour the milk over the mushrooms and bring to a simmer. Add the cockles or mussels, samphire and potato.

4 Heat through the contents of the saucepan and then ladle into four deep ovenproof soup bowls. Add a sprig of thyme to each.

5 Moisten the edges of the bowls with beaten egg, cover with the pastry rounds and press the edges to seal. Brush with more beaten egg, sprinkle with sesame seeds and bake in the oven for 35–40 minutes until the pastry top is puffed and golden.

Cook's Tip

Closed button or Cremini mushrooms can be substituted.

Fresh Tuna Shiitake Teriyaki

Teriyaki is a sweet soy marinade usually used to glaze meat. Here Teriyaki enhances fresh tuna steaks served with rich shiitake mushrooms.

SERVES 4

4 × 6oz fresh blue fin or yellow tail steaks
salt
⅔ cup Teriyaki sauce
6 oz / 1¾ cups shiitake mushrooms, sliced
8 oz white radish, peeled
2 large carrots, peeled

1 Season the tuna steaks with a sprinkling of salt, then set aside for 20 minutes for it to penetrate. Pour the Teriyaki sauce over the fish and mushrooms and marinate for another 20–30 minutes or longer if you have the time.

Cook's Tip
A good Teriyaki sauce is made by Kikkoman and can be found in most large supermarkets.

2 Preheat a moderate broiler or barbecue grill. Remove the tuna from marinade and reserve the marinade. Cook the tuna for 8 minutes, turning once.

3 Transfer the mushrooms and marinade to a stainless steel saucepan and simmer for 3–4 minutes.

4 Slice the radish and carrot thinly then shred finely with a chopping knife. Arrange in heaps on four serving plates and add the fish, with the mushrooms and sauce poured over. Serve with plain boiled rice.

Turbans of Lemon Sole with a Paris Mushroom Twist

The Paris mushroom *champignon de Paris* or Cremini mushroom is the French equivalent of the English white button mushroom. Its mild woodland flavor goes well with the lemon sole.

SERVES 4

2 lb lemon sole, filleted and skinned to yield 1 lb of fish
5 tbsp dry white wine
½ cup water
3½ tbsp heavy cream
2 tsp cornstarch
2 tsp lemon juice
celery salt and cayenne pepper

For the Mushroom Filling

4 tbsp unsalted butter, plus extra for greasing
1 shallot, finely chopped
6 oz / 1¾ cups Cremini or oyster mushrooms, finely chopped
1 tbsp chopped fresh thyme
salt and freshly ground black pepper

1 Preheat the oven to 375°F and butter an ovenproof casserole. Make the mushroom filling. Melt the butter in a frying pan and sauté the shallot until it is soft.

Cook's Tip
If planning ahead, the fish can be rolled and kept ready to cook for up to 8 hours.

2 Add the mushrooms and thyme and cook until dry. Transfer to a bowl, season and allow to cool.

3 Lay the fish skin side uppermost, season and spread with the filling. Roll up each fillet, then place in the buttered dish.

4 Pour in the wine and water, then cover with a piece of buttered wax paper and cook in the oven for approximately 20 minutes.

5 Transfer the fish to a warmed serving platter and strain the cooking juices into a small saucepan. Add the cream and bring to a simmer.

6 Blend the cornstarch with 1 tbsp of water, add to the pan, stir and simmer to thicken, then add the lemon juice and season with celery salt and a pinch of cayenne pepper. Pour the sauce around the fish and serve with new potatoes, beans and carrots.

Truffle and Lobster Risotto

To capture the precious qualities of the fresh truffle, partner it with lobster and serve in a silky smooth risotto. Both truffle shavings and truffle oil are added towards the end of cooking to preserve their flavor.

SERVES 4

4 tbsp unsalted butter
1 medium onion, chopped
2 cups Arborio or other short-grain rice
1 sprig thyme
5 cups chicken broth
⅔ cup dry white wine
1 freshly cooked lobster
3 tbsp chopped fresh parsley and chervil
3–4 drops truffle oil
2 hard-boiled eggs, sliced
1 fresh black or white truffle

1 Melt the butter in a large shallow pan, add the onion and fry gently until soft without letting it color. Add the rice and thyme and stir well to coat evenly with fat. Pour in the chicken broth and wine, stir once and cook uncovered for 15 minutes.

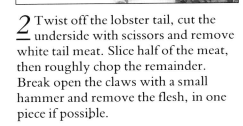

2 Twist off the lobster tail, cut the underside with scissors and remove white tail meat. Slice half of the meat, then roughly chop the remainder. Break open the claws with a small hammer and remove the flesh, in one piece if possible.

3 Remove the rice from the heat, stir in the chopped lobster meat, herbs and truffle oil. Cover and let stand for 5 minutes.

Cook's Tip
To make the most of the aromatic truffle scent, keep the tuber in the rice jar for a few days. Alternatively store with the eggs at room temperature.

4 Divide among warmed dishes and arrange the lobster and hard-boiled egg slices and shavings of fresh truffle on top. Serve immediately.

Creamy Fish and Mushroom Pie

Fish pie is a healthy and hearty dish for a hungry family. To help the fish go further, mushrooms provide both flavor and nourishment.

SERVES 4

8 oz / 2½ cups assorted wild and cultivated mushrooms such as oyster, button, chanterelle or chicken of the woods, trimmed and quartered

1½ lb cod or haddock fillet, skinned and diced

2½ cups milk, boiling

For the Topping

2 lb floury potatoes, peeled and quartered

2 tbsp butter

⅔ cup milk

salt and freshly ground black pepper

grated nutmeg

For the Sauce

4 tbsp unsalted butter

1 medium onion, chopped

½ celery stalk, chopped

½ cup all-purpose flour

2 tsp lemon juice

3 tbsp chopped fresh parsley

4 Slowly add the reserved liquid, stirring until absorbed. Return to the heat, stir and simmer to thicken. Add the lemon juice and parsley, season, then add to the baking pan.

1 Preheat the oven to 400°F. Butter an ovenproof casserole, sprinkle the mushrooms over the bottom, add the fish and season with salt and pepper. Pour on the boiling milk, cover and cook in the oven for 20 minutes. Using a slotted spoon, transfer the fish and mushrooms to a 6¼ cup baking pan. Pour the poaching liquid into a small pitcher and set aside.

2 Cover the potatoes with cold water, add a good pinch of salt and boil for 20 minutes. Drain and mash with the butter and milk. Season well.

3 To make the sauce, melt the butter in a saucepan, add the onion and celery and fry until soft but not colored. Stir in the flour, then remove from the heat.

5 Top with the mashed potato and return to the oven for 30–40 minutes until golden brown.

Pan-fried Salmon with a Tarragon Mushroom Sauce

Tarragon has a distinctive aniseed flavour that is good with fish, cream and mushrooms. This recipe uses oyster mushrooms to provide both texture and flavor.

SERVES 4

4 tbsp unsalted butter
salt and cayenne pepper
4 × 6 oz salmon steaks
1 shallot, finely chopped
6 oz / 1⅓ cups assorted wild and cultivated mushrooms such as oyster mushrooms, saffron milk-caps, bay boletes or cauliflower fungus, trimmed and sliced
⅞ cup chicken or vegetable stock
2 tsp cornstarch
½ tsp mustard
3½ tbsp sour cream
3 tbsp chopped fresh tarragon
1 tsp white wine vinegar

Cook's Tip
Fresh tarragon will bruise and darken quickly after chopping, so prepare the herb as and when you need it.

1 Melt half of the butter in a large non-stick frying pan, season the salmon and cook over a moderate heat for 8 minutes, turning once. Transfer to a plate, cover and keep warm.

2 Heat the remaining butter in the pan and gently fry the shallot to soften without letting it color. Add the mushrooms and cook until the juices begin to flow. Add the stock and simmer for 2–3 minutes.

3 Put the cornstarch and mustard in a cup and blend with 1 tbsp of water. Stir into the mushroom mixture and bring to a simmer, stirring, to thicken. Add the cream, tarragon, vinegar and salt and cayenne pepper.

4 Spoon the mushrooms over each salmon steak and serve with new potatoes and a green salad.

Fillets of Sole Bonne Femme

To capture the delicate flavor of flat fish, it is best cooked simply with wine and few good mushrooms.

SERVES 4

½ cup unsalted butter
1 shallot, finely chopped
5 oz / 1½ cups chanterelles, Cremini or button mushrooms, trimmed and sliced
2 lb lemon sole, skinned and filleted to yield approximately 1 lb of fish
salt and cayenne pepper
5 tbsp dry white wine
⅞ cup homemade or canned fish or chicken broth
1 tsp lemon juice
2 lb potatoes, peeled, boiled and mashed
1 tbsp chopped fresh Italian parsley, to garnish

1 Preheat the oven to 325°F. Sauté the shallot in 2 tbsp of the butter until soft. Turn into an ovenproof earthenware casserole and add the mushrooms. Place the fish fillets on top and season lightly.

2 Pour in the wine and broth and cover with buttered wax paper. Cook in the oven for 25 minutes.

3 Transfer to a flameproof serving dish and keep warm. Strain the liquid into a shallow frying pan, reserving the mushrooms and shallot. Boil the sauce rapidly until reduced to a syrupy liquid. Remove from the heat, add the remaining butter cut into small pieces and shake the pan (the sauce must not boil). Add the mushroom mixture, the lemon juice and seasoning.

4 Heat the broiler to a moderate temperature. Pipe a border of potatoes around the dish, spoon the sauce over and heat under the broiler.

Shrimp and Mushroom Kebabs

The flavor of grilled or barbecued shrimp combines especially well with chanterelles, chicken of the woods and saffron milk-caps. The mushrooms need to be blanched and then moistened with oil to prevent them from burning over the coals.

SERVES 4

6 oz / 1¾ cups wild mushrooms such as chanterelles, chicken of the woods, saffron milk caps, or shiitake, trimmed and cut into pieces
3 tbsp olive oil
12 large raw shrimp
1 fennel bulb, thickly sliced
8 cherry tomatoes
celery salt and cayenne pepper

1 Preheat a moderate broiler or barbecue. Bring a saucepan of water to a boil, and blanch the mushrooms for 30 seconds. Transfer to a bowl with a slotted spoon and add a little oil.

Cook's Tip
Buy fresh raw shrimp if you can, they taste much better than frozen.

2 Moisten the shrimp with a little more oil, then thread onto four metal skewers alternating with the pieces of fennel, tomatoes and mushrooms.

3 Season lightly, then broil for 6–8 minutes, turning once. Serve on a bed of long grain and wild rice with a simple green salad.

Fruits of the Sea and Forest in Puff Pastry

The freshest fish and the finest wild mushrooms are combined here in a delicious cream sauce. The spectacular puff pastry shell is easier to make than it looks.

SERVES 4

12 oz puff pastry, thawed if frozen
1 egg, beaten, to glaze
⅞ cup dry white wine
1 cup homemade or canned chicken or vegetable broth
12 oz / 3½ cups assorted wild and cultivated mushrooms such as oyster, chanterelles, shiitake, hedgehog fungus, cauliflower fungus, saffron milk-caps, chicken of the woods or St George's mushrooms, trimmed and cut into thumb-sized pieces
1 medium squid
4 oz monkfish, boned and cut into large pieces
12 mussels in their shells, scrubbed
8 oz salmon fillet, skinned and cut into bite-sized pieces
12 large raw shrimp, peeled
6 sea scallops, halved
4 tbsp unsalted butter
2 shallots, finely chopped
4 tbsp all-purpose flour
5 tbsp crème fraîche
2 tsp lemon juice
salt and cayenne pepper

1 Roll out the pastry on a floured surface to form a rectangle 12 × 15 in. Cut out a 9 in circle and place on a baking sheet. Prick all over with a fork and brush the surface with beaten egg. Cut out 1½ in circles with a fluted pastry cutter. Overlap these shapes around the edge of the large circle, brush again with egg and chill for 1 hour in a fridge. Preheat the oven to 400°F.

5 Bring the wine and broth to a simmer and add the squid, monkfish, mussels, salmon, shrimp and scallops and cook for 6 minutes. Remove with a slotted spoon and add to the bowl with the mushrooms. Discard any mussels which have not opened. Strain the cooking liquid and make up to 1½ cups with water, if necessary. Bake the pastry for 25–30 minutes until golden.

2 Bring the wine and broth to a simmer, add the mushrooms and cook gently for 3–4 minutes. Remove with a slotted spoon and set aside in a large bowl.

6 Melt the butter in a saucepan, add the shallots and fry gently until soft but not colored. Stir in the flour and remove from the heat. Gradually add the broth to make a smooth sauce and then return to the heat and simmer to thicken, stirring frequently.

3 To prepare the squid, pull the head and tentacles away from the body, sever the tentacles and chop coarsely. Remove the quill from inside the body, pull off the side fins and set aside. Rinse the body piece under water and rub off the fine outer skin. Cut the body piece in half lengthways, open out and score a criss-cross pattern with a sharp knife over the inside surface. Cut the squid into wide strips.

7 Add the crème fraîche and then stir in the mushrooms and fish. Add the lemon juice and season to taste. Spoon the mixture into the pastry shell and serve with buttered parsley potatoes and spring vegetables. There will be enough filling for an extra serving.

4 Tap the mussels sharply and discard any that do not close.

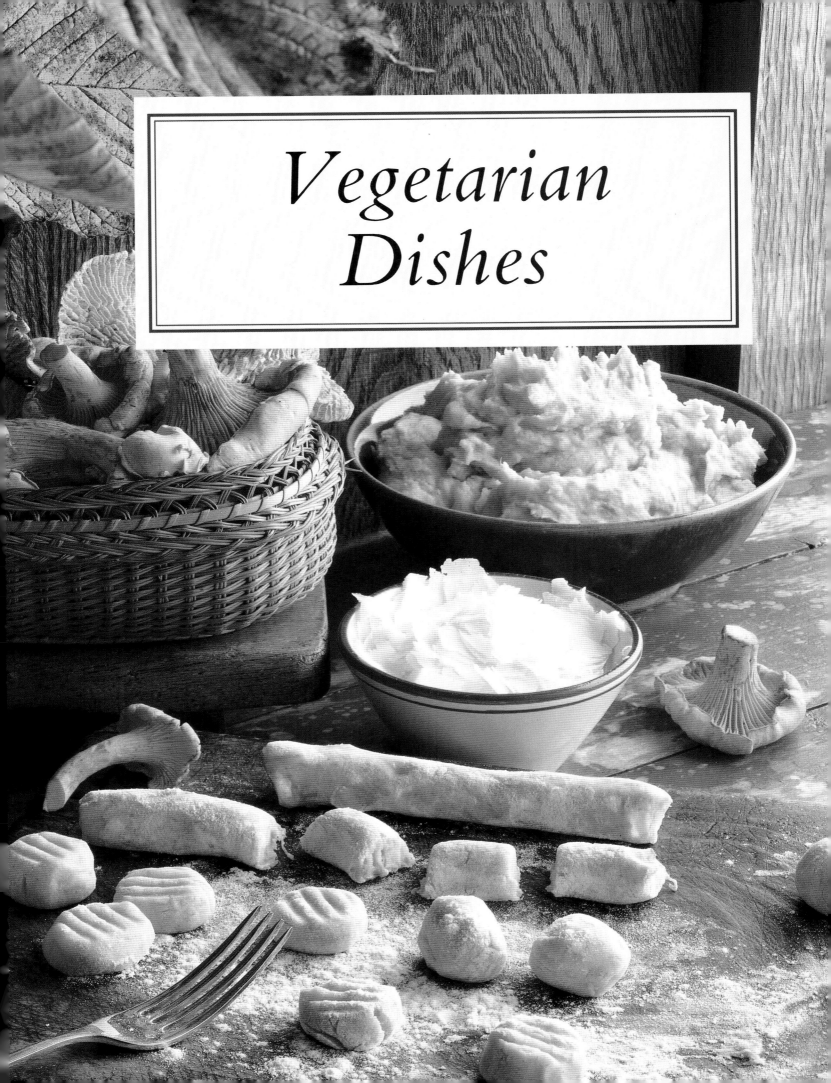

Vegetarian Dishes

Wild Mushroom Brioche with an Orange Butter Sauce

The finest wild mushrooms deserve the best treatment. Try this butter-rich brioche stuffed full of flavorsome fungi.

SERVES 4

1 tsp active dried yeast
3 tbsp milk, at room temperature
3½ cups white all-purpose flour
1 tsp salt
1 tbsp superfine sugar
3 eggs
finely grated rind of ½ lemon
⅞ cup unsalted butter, at room temperature

For the Filling

4 tbsp unsalted butter
2 shallots, chopped
12 oz / 3½ cups assorted wild and cultivated mushrooms, such as ceps, bay boletes, chanterelles, winter chanterelles, saffron milk-caps, oyster mushrooms and horn of plenty, trimmed, sliced and roughly chopped
½ garlic clove, crushed
5 tbsp chopped fresh parsley
salt and freshly ground black pepper

For the Orange Butter Sauce

2 tbsp frozen orange juice concentrate
¾ cup unsalted butter, diced
salt and cayenne pepper

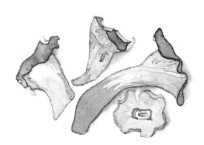

1 Dissolve the yeast in the milk, add 1 cup of the flour and mix to form a dough. Fill a bowl with warm water, then place the dough in the water. Leave for 30 minutes in a warm place to activate the yeast.

2 Place the remaining 2½ cups of flour in the bowl of a food processor fitted with the dough or metal blade and add the salt, sugar, eggs, lemon rind and the risen dough and process briefly to mix. Add the diced butter and process until the dough is silky smooth and very elastic. Lift the dough out onto a sheet of plastic wrap and refrigerate for 2 hours until firm. Meanwhile, preheat the oven to 375°F.

3 Sauté the shallots in the butter without letting them brown. Add the mushrooms and garlic, allow the juices to run and then increase the heat to reduce the moisture. When dry, turn into a bowl, add the parsley, season well and allow to cool.

4 Grease and line a 2 lb loaf tin with non-stick wax paper. Roll the brioche out on a floured surface to form a rectangle 6 × 12 in. Spoon the cooked mushrooms over the dough and roll up to make a fat sausage. Drop the dough into the loaf pan, cover with a damp dish towel and leave to rise in a warm humid place for 50 minutes. When the dough has risen above the level of the rim, place in the oven and bake for 40 minutes.

5 To make the sauce, place the orange juice concentrate in a heatproof glass bowl and heat by standing in a saucepan of simmering water. Remove the pan from the heat, and gradually whisk in the butter until creamy. Season to taste, cover and keep warm. When the brioche is cooked, turn it out, slice and serve with orange butter sauce and a simple green salad.

Cook's Tip

Allow plenty of time for this recipe. It helps to make the dough and filling ahead and chill them until needed.

Mushroom Picker's Omelet

Enthusiastic mushroom pickers have been known to carry with them a portable gas stove, an omelet pan and a few eggs, ready to assemble an on-site brunch.

SERVES 1

2 tbsp unsalted butter, plus extra for cooking

4 oz / 1¼ cups assorted wild and cultivated mushrooms such as young ceps, bay boletes, chanterelles, saffron milk-caps, closed field mushrooms, oyster mushrooms, hedgehog and matsatake mushrooms, trimmed and sliced

3 eggs, at room temperature

salt and freshly ground black pepper

1 Melt the butter in a small omelet pan, add the mushrooms and cook until the juices run. Season, remove from pan and set aside. Wipe the pan.

2 Break the eggs into a bowl, season and beat with a fork. Heat the omelet pan over a high heat, add a pat of butter and let it begin to brown. Pour in the beaten egg and stir briskly with the back of a fork.

3 When the eggs are two-thirds scrambled, add the mushrooms and let the omelet finish cooking for 10–15 seconds.

Cook's Tip

From start to finish, an omelet should be cooked and on the table in less than a minute. For best results use farm fresh eggs at room temperature.

4 Tap the handle of the omelet pan sharply with your fist to loosen the omelet from the pan, then fold and turn onto a plate. Serve with warm crusty bread and a simple green salad.

Open Cap Mushrooms Stuffed with Hummus and Herbs

The up-turned cap of the field mushroom provides an ideal resting place for a spoonful of hummus; made here from canned chick-peas.

SERVES 4

12 medium open cap field mushrooms
4 tbsp olive oil
2 tbsp lemon juice
For the Hummus
14 oz can chick-peas, drained
2 tbsp tahini
2 garlic cloves, crushed
5 tbsp olive oil
celery salt and cayenne pepper
6 tbsp chopped fresh parsley
2 tbsp mild paprika
stuffed olives, to garnish

Cook's Tip
Tahini is a thick paste made from sesame seeds. It can be found in Middle Eastern food stores and most large supermarkets.

1 Preheat the oven to 375°F. Meanwhile, snap off the mushroom stems at the base and save for use in another recipe.

2 Combine the olive oil with 2 tsp lemon juice in a cup and liberally brush over the insides of the mushroom caps. Arrange on a baking sheet and cook in the oven for 25 minutes. Allow to cool.

3 To make the hummus, blend the chick-peas in a food processor until smooth, add the tahini, garlic and olive oil. Process well, then season with celery salt and cayenne pepper.

4 Spoon the hummus into the mushroom cups, then mold into cone shapes, mask one side with the chopped parsley and dust the other with mild paprika. Serve at room temperature garnished with the olives, with bread and pickled green peppers.

Creamy Beet and Potato Gratin with Wild Mushrooms

Polish communities make the most of robust flavors in their cooking and are often first in the woods when mushrooms appear. This inexpensive dish captures the spirit of their autumn menus.

SERVES 4

2 tbsp vegetable oil
1 medium onion, chopped
3 tbsp all-purpose flour
1¼ cups vegetable broth
1½ lb cooked beets, peeled and chopped
5 tbsp light cream
2 tbsp horseradish sauce
1 tsp hot mustard
1 tbsp wine vinegar
1 tsp caraway seeds
2 tbsp unsalted butter
1 shallot, chopped
8 oz / 2½ cups assorted wild and cultivated mushrooms such as ceps, bay boletes, chanterelles, chicken of the woods, blewits, fairy ring, parasol, oyster, field, shiitake, hen of the woods and honey mushrooms, trimmed and sliced
3 tbsp chopped fresh parsley

For the Potato Border

2 lb floury potatoes, peeled
⅔ cup milk
1 tbsp chopped fresh dill (optional)
salt and freshly ground black pepper

1 Preheat the oven to 375°F. Lightly oil a 9 in round baking dish. Heat the oil in a large saucepan, add the onion and sauté until soft without coloring. Stir in the flour, remove from the heat and gradually add the broth, stirring until well blended.

2 Return to the heat, stir and simmer to thicken, then add the beets, cream, horseradish, mustard, vinegar and caraway seeds.

3 Bring the potatoes to a boil in salted water and cook for 20 minutes. Drain well and mash with the milk. Add the dill if using and season to taste with salt and pepper.

4 Spoon the potatoes into the prepared dish and make a well in the center. Spoon the beet mixture into the well and set aside.

5 Melt the butter in a large nonstick frying pan and sauté the shallot until soft, without browning. Add the mushrooms and cook over a moderate heat until their juices begin to run. Increase the heat and boil off the moisture. When dry, season and stir in the chopped parsley. Spread the mushrooms over the beet mixture, cover and bake for 30 minutes.

Cook's Tip

If planning ahead, this entire dish can be made in advance and heated through when needed. Allow 50 minutes baking time from room temperature.

Chicken of the Woods Saté with a Spiced Hazelnut Sauce

To capture the texture and flavor of chicken of the woods, marinate them in a rich hazelnut sauce.

SERVES 4

12 oz / 3½ cups chicken of the woods, trimmed and diced
½ cup hazelnuts, toasted
1 shallot, quartered
2 oz crustless white bread
2 tbsp hazelnut or olive oil
1⅞ cup boiling vegetable broth, homemade or canned
¼ tsp ground cinnamon
1 tsp honey
grated rind and juice of ½ small orange
½ tsp celery salt
¼ tsp cayenne pepper

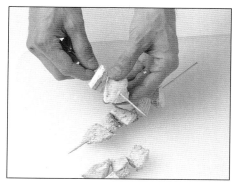

1 Cover the chicken of the woods with boiling water and leave for 2–3 minutes to soften. Thread onto bamboo skewers and set aside.

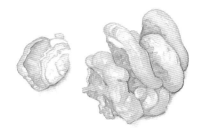

2 Grind the hazelnuts in a food processor, add the shallot and process until smooth. Add the bread, oil, broth, cinnamon, honey, rind and juice. Blend again, then season to taste with celery salt and cayenne pepper.

3 Spoon half of the marinade over the skewered chicken of the woods and set aside at room temperature for 30–40 minutes. Preheat a moderate broiler and cook for 8 minutes, turning once.

4 Serve with couscous or rice, green salad and the remaining sauce, warm or at room temperature.

Cook's Tip
Young chicken of the woods is best suited for this recipe. Older fungi tend to dry with age.

Savoy Cabbage Stuffed with Mushroom Barley

The veined texture of savoy cabbage provides good cover for an earthy rich stuffing of barley and wild mushrooms.

SERVES 4

4 tbsp unsalted butter
2 medium onions, chopped
1 celery stalk, sliced
8 oz / 2½ cups assorted wild and cultivated mushrooms such as young ceps, bay boletes, closed shaggy ink caps, chicken of the woods, saffron milk-caps, amethyst deceivers, oyster and closed field mushrooms, and blewits, trimmed, sliced and roughly chopped, or 2 tbsp dried ceps, bay boletes or saffron milk-caps, soaked in warm water for 20 minutes, and 7 oz / 2 cups Cremini mushrooms, roughly chopped
1¼ cups pearl barley
1 sprig fresh thyme
3⅔ cups water
2 tbsp almond or cashew nut butter
½ vegetable stock cube
salt and freshly ground black pepper
1 savoy cabbage

Cook's Tip
A range of nut butters is available in all leading health food stores.

1 Melt the butter in a large heavy saucepan, add the onions and celery and sauté for 6–8 minutes until soft. Add the mushrooms and cook until they release their juices, then add the barley, thyme, water and the nut butter. Bring to a boil, cover and simmer for 30 minutes. Add the ½ stock cube and simmer for a further 20 minutes. Season to taste.

2 Separate the cabbage leaves and cut away the thick stem. Blanch the leaves in salted boiling water for 3–4 minutes. Drain and refresh under cold running water. Drain again.

3 Lay an 18in piece of cheesecloth over a steamer. Reconstruct the cabbage by lining the cheesecloth with large cabbage leaves. Spread a layer of mushroom barley over the leaves.

4 Cover with a second layer of leaves and filling. Continue until the center is full. Draw together opposite corners of the cheesecloth and tie firmly. Place the cabbage in a steamer, set in a saucepan containing 1 in of simmering water, cover and steam for 30 minutes. To serve, place on a warmed serving plate, untie the cheesecloth and carefully pull it out from underneath the cabbage.

Cook's Tip
If planning ahead, the cabbage can be assembled well in advance before the final cooking. To ensure richness and flavor use a good portion of ceps, chicken of the woods and field mushrooms.

Mushroom Picker's Pâté

A good vegetarian pâté should be as smooth and as rich as one made with fine liver. This recipe compares very favorably to traditional meat ones.

SERVES 4

3 tbsp vegetable oil
1 medium onion, chopped
½ celery stick, chopped
12 oz / 3½ cups assorted wild and cultivated mushrooms such as closed field mushrooms, fairy ring, oyster and shiitake mushrooms, bay bolete and horn of plenty, trimmed and sliced
⅔ cup red lentils
2¼ cups homemade or canned vegetable broth or water
1 sprig thyme
4 tbsp almond or cashew nut butter
1 garlic clove, crushed
1 oz bread, crusts removed
5 tbsp milk
1 tbsp lemon juice
4 egg yolks
celery salt and freshly ground black pepper

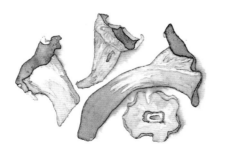

1 Preheat the oven to 350°F. Heat the oil in a large saucepan, add the onion and celery and brown lightly. Add the mushrooms and sauté for 3–4 minutes. Remove a spoonful of the mushroom pieces and set aside until they are needed.

2 Add the lentils, stock and thyme, bring to a boil uncovered and simmer for 20 minutes or until the lentils have fallen apart.

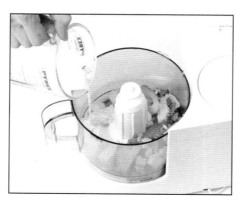

3 Place the nut butter, garlic, bread and milk in a food processor and blend until smooth.

4 Add the lemon juice and egg yolks and combine. Add the lentil mixture, blend, then season well. Lastly stir the reserved mushrooms into the mixture.

5 Turn the mixture into a 5 cup pâté or loaf pan, stand in a roasting pan half filled with boiling water, cover and cook for 50 minutes. Allow to cool before serving from the pan.

Cook's Tip

If you are using only cultivated mushrooms, an addition of ⅓ oz / 3 tbsp of dried ceps, bay boletes, chanterelles and horn of plenty will provide a good wild mushroom flavor. Soak first in warm water for 20 minutes.

Almond or cashew nut butter is available from most good health food shops.

Japanese Mushrooms with Lemon and Walnut Noodles

The flavor of the Japanese enokitaki mushroom is as fine as its appearance. This preparation captures their sweet peppery taste. If quail eggs are un-obtainable, substitute the smallest chicken eggs.

SERVES 4

1/3 cup somen noodles or vermicelli pasta

1 large carrot, peeled, sliced and shredded

2¼ cups dashi, or light vegetable broth, made with a cube

½ oz arame or hijiki dried seaweed

2 oz / ¾ cup enokitaki mushrooms

1 tsp lemon juice

2 tsp walnut oil

1 scallion, green part only, sliced

1 Cook the noodles and carrots in salted boiling water for 3–4 minutes. Drain, cool under running water and set aside.

Cook's Tip
The enokitaki mushroom is a cultivated variety and is available from Japanese supermarkets worldwide. Dried seaweed and somen noodles can be found in most health food stores.

2 Bring the dashi or stock to the boil, add the arame or seaweed and simmer for 2 minutes. Add the noodles, mushrooms, lemon juice and oil and briefly reheat.

3 Divide among four Japanese soup bowls, sprinkle with scallion slices and serve.

Late Summer Mushrooms and Vegetables in a Hazelnut Dressing

Seasonal flavors merge well with autumn mushrooms to give this vegetable dish distinctive character.

SERVES 4

2 tbsp vegetable oil

1 shallot, chopped

1 celery stalk, sliced

8 oz / 2½ cups assorted wild and cultivated mushrooms such as young ceps, bay boletes, chanterelles, amethyst deceivers, horn of plenty, oyster, shiitake, queen boletes, Caesar's mushrooms and honey mushrooms, trimmed, sliced or halved if small

salt and freshly ground black pepper

6 oz small potatoes, scrubbed or scraped

1 cup young green beans, trimmed and halved

4 oz baby carrots, trimmed and peeled

1 cup fava beans

3 tbsp hazelnut oil

1 tbsp peanut oil

1 tbsp lemon juice

1 tsp chopped fresh thyme

2 oz hazelnuts, toasted and chopped

1 Sauté the shallot and celery in vegetable oil until soft but without coloring. Add the mushrooms and cook over a moderate heat until their juices begin to run, then increase the heat to boil off the juices. Season and set aside.

2 In separate pans, boil the potatoes for 20 minutes, beans and carrots for 6 minutes and the fava beans for 3 minutes. Drain and cool under running water, then remove the tough outer skins of the fava beans.

3 Combine the vegetables with the mushrooms, then moisten with hazelnut and peanut oil. Add the lemon juice and thyme, season and sprinkle with toasted hazelnuts.

Wild Mushroom Gratin with Fontina Cheese, New Potatoes, Pickles and Walnuts

This gratin is one of the simplest and most delicious ways of cooking mushrooms. The dish is inspired by the Swiss custom of eating alpine cheeses with new potatoes and small cornichons.

SERVES 4

2 lb new potatoes, scrubbed or scraped

4 tbsp unsalted butter or 4 tbsp olive oil

12 oz / 3½ cups assorted wild and cultivated mushrooms such as oyster, shiitake and closed field mushrooms, ceps, bay boletes, chanterelles, winter chanterelles, hedgehog fungus, matsutake mushrooms and saffron milk-caps

salt and freshly ground black pepper

6 oz Fontina cheese

½ cup walnut or pecan pieces, toasted

12 medium cornichons and mixed green salad leaves, to serve

1 Place the potatoes in a pan of salted water, bring to a boil and cook for 20 minutes. Drain, add the pat of butter, cover and keep warm.

2 Trim the mushrooms and then slice them thinly.

3 Sauté the mushrooms in the remaining butter or oil. When the juices appear, increase the heat to evaporate the moisture.

4 Preheat a moderate broiler. Slice the cheese thinly, arrange on top of the mushroom slices and broil until bubbly and brown. Sprinkle with walnuts and serve with buttered new potatoes, cornichons and a green salad.

Cook's Tip

For best results, choose an attractive flameproof dish that can be put under the broiler and brought directly to the table.

Hash Brown Chicken of the Woods with Potatoes and Onions

This hash brown dinner is a very special treat. It calls for the intriguing *Laetiporus sulphureus*, or chicken of the woods, which looks, tastes and has the texture of chicken, and that undefinable extra of wild mushroom.

SERVES 4

2 lb potatoes, peeled
4 tbsp unsalted butter
2 medium onions, sliced
1 celery stalk, sliced
1 small carrot, peeled and cut into small slices
8 oz chicken of the woods, trimmed and sliced
3 tbsp medium sherry
3 tbsp chopped fresh parsley
1 tbsp chopped fresh chives
grated rind of ½ lemon
salt and freshly ground black pepper

1 Place the potatoes in a saucepan of salted water, bring to a boil and cook for 20 minutes. Drain, cool and slice thickly.

Cook's Tip
The best hash browns are made from late season floury potatoes that are inclined to fall apart when cooked. This quality helps the mixture to form a more solid mass in the pan.

2 Melt the butter in a large nonstick frying pan, add the onions, celery and carrot and sauté until lightly browned.

3 Add the chicken of the woods and the sherry, then simmer to evaporate any moisture.

4 Add the potatoes, herbs, lemon rind and seasoning, toss and fry together until crispy brown. Serve with a salad of frisée and young spinach leaves.

Mushroom Börek

The Turkish *börek* is a rich pastry package with various savory fillings, such as the following.

SERVES 4

⅓ cup couscous
3 tbsp olive oil
1 medium onion, chopped
8 oz / 2½ cups assorted wild and cultivated mushrooms such as ceps, bay boletes, chanterelles, winter chanterelles, oyster, field and Caesar's mushrooms, trimmed and sliced
1 garlic clove, crushed
4 tbsp chopped fresh parsley
1 tsp chopped fresh thyme
1 egg, hard-boiled and peeled
salt and freshly ground black pepper

For the Börek Pastry

3½ cups self-rising flour
1 tsp salt
1 egg, plus extra for glazing
⅔ cup plain yogurt
⅔ cup olive oil
grated rind of ½ lemon

For the Yogurt Sauce

⅞ cup plain yogurt
3 tbsp chopped fresh mint
½ tsp superfine sugar
¼ tsp cayenne pepper
¼ tsp celery salt
a little milk or water

1 Preheat the oven to 375°F. Just cover the couscous with boiling water and soak for 10 minutes or until the liquid is absorbed. Then sauté the onion in oil without letting it color. Add the mushrooms and garlic and cook until the juices begin to run, then increase the heat to evaporate the juices. Transfer to a bowl, add the parsley, thyme and couscous and stir well. Chop the hard-boiled egg into the mixture, season and combine.

2 To make the pastry, sift the flour and salt into a bowl. Make a well, add the egg, yogurt, olive oil and lemon rind and combine with a fork.

3 Turn out onto a floured surface and roll into a 12 in circle. Pile the mixture into the center of the pastry, and bring the edges over, to enclose the filling. Turn upside down onto a baking sheet. Press the börek out flat with your hand, glaze with beaten egg and bake for 25 minutes.

4 To make the sauce, blend the yogurt with the mint, sugar, cayenne pepper and celery salt, adjusting the consistency with milk or water. Serve börek at room temperature.

Egg and Rice Cakes with Sour Cream and Mushrooms

SERVES 4

1 egg
1 tbsp all-purpose flour
4 tbsp freshly grated Parmesan, Fontina or Pecorino cheese
2 cups cooked long grain rice
salt and freshly ground black pepper
4 tbsp unsalted butter, plus extra for frying
1 shallot or small onion, chopped
6 oz / 1¾ cups assorted wild and cultivated mushrooms such as ceps, bay boletes, chanterelles, winter chanterelles, horn of plenty, blewits, field and oyster mushrooms, trimmed and sliced
1 sprig thyme

2 tbsp Madeira or sherry
⅔ cup sour cream or crème fraîche
paprika for dusting (optional)

1 Beat the egg, flour and cheese together with a fork, then stir in the cooked rice. Mix well and set aside.

2 Sauté the shallot or onion in half the butter until soft but not brown. Add the mushrooms and thyme and cook until the juices run. Add the Madeira or sherry. Increase the heat to reduce the juices and concentrate the flavor. Season to taste, transfer to a bowl, cover and keep warm.

3 Fry spoonsful of the rice mixture in a pat of butter. Cook each one for a minute on each side. When all the rice cakes are cooked, arrange on four warmed plates, top with sour cream or crème fraîche and a spoonful of mushrooms. Dust with paprika and serve with asparagus and baby carrots.

Pumpkin Gnocchi with a Chanterelle Parsley Cream

Gnocchi is an Italian pasta dumpling usually made from potatoes, in this special recipe, pumpkin is added, too. A chanterelle sauce provides both richness and flavor.

SERVES 4

1 lb peeled floury potatoes
1 lb peeled pumpkin, chopped
2 egg yolks
1¾ cups all-purpose flour, plus more if necessary
pinch of ground allspice
¼ tsp ground cinnamon
pinch of grated nutmeg
finely grated rind of ½ orange
salt and freshly ground pepper

For the Sauce

2 tbsp olive oil
1 shallot
6 oz / 2 cups fresh chanterelles, sliced, or ½ oz / ¼ cup dried, soaked for 20 minutes in warm water
2 tsp almond butter
⅔ cup crème fraîche
a little milk or water
5 tbsp chopped fresh parsley
½ cup grated Parmesan or Romano cheese

Cook's Tip
If planning ahead, gnocchi can be shaped ready for cooking up to 8 hours in advance. Almond butter is available ready-made from health food shops.

1 Cover the potatoes with cold salted water, bring to a boil and cook for 20 minutes. Drain and set aside. Place the pumpkin in a bowl, cover and microwave on full power for 8 minutes. Alternatively, wrap the pumpkin in foil and bake at 350°F for 30 minutes. Drain well, then add to the potato and pass through a vegetable mill into a bowl. Add the egg yolks, flour, spices, orange rind and seasoning and mix well to make a soft dough. Add more flour if the mixture is too loose.

2 Bring a large pan of salted water to the boil, then lightly cover a work surface with all-purpose flour. Spoon the gnocchi mixture into an icing bag fitted with a ½ in plain nozzle. Pipe onto the floured surface to make a 6 in sausage. Roll in flour and cut into 1 in pieces. Repeat the process making more sausage shapes. Mark each lightly with a fork and cook for 3–4 minutes in the boiling water.

3 Meanwhile, make the sauce. Heat the oil in a nonstick frying pan, add the shallot and fry until soft without coloring. Add the chanterelles and cook briefly, then add the almond butter. Stir to melt and stir in the crème fraîche. Simmer briefly and adjust the consistency with milk or water. Add the parsley and season to taste.

4 Lift the gnocchi out of the water with a slotted spoon, turn into bowls and spoon the sauce over the top. Sprinkle with Parmesan cheese.

Goat Cheese Kasha with Ceps and Walnuts

Kasha is a Russian staple of cooked grains. Robustly flavored buckwheat is most common and is often combined with other grains. Couscous is used here and allows the flavor of buckwheat, goat cheese, dried ceps and toasted walnuts to come through.

SERVES 4

1 cup couscous
3 tbsp buckwheat
15 g / ¼ cup dried ceps or bay boletes
3 eggs
4 tbsp chopped fresh parsley
2 tsp chopped fresh thyme
4 tbsp olive oil
3 tbsp walnut oil
1½ cups crumbly white goat cheese
½ cup walnut pieces, toasted
salt and freshly ground black pepper
salad and rye bread, to serve

Cook's Tip
The flavor of buckwheat may be too strong for some tastes. In this case replace with couscous. Kasha can also be made from bulgur wheat or millet.

1 Place the couscous, buckwheat and ceps in a bowl, cover with boiling water and let soak for 15 minutes. Drain off any excess liquid.

3 Stir in the parsley, thyme, olive oil, walnut oil, goat cheese and walnuts. Season to taste with salt and pepper.

2 Place the mixture in a large nonstick frying pan, add the eggs, season well, then scramble with a flat wooden spoon over a moderate heat.

4 Transfer to a large serving dish and serve hot with rye bread, salad and Eastern European beer if available.

INDEX